He walked by faith and not by sight,
　By love and not by law ;
The presence of the wrong or right
　He rather felt than saw.

And, pausing not for doubtful choice,
　Of evils great or small,
He listened to that inner voice
　Which called away from all.

O Spirit of that early day,
　So pure and strong and true,
Be with us in the narrow way
　Our faithful fathers knew.

Give strength the evil to forsake,
　The cross of truth to bear,
And love and reverent fear to make
　Our daily lives a prayer.
　　　　　　　　　　　WHITTIER

FIVE "MUSTS"
OF THE
CHRISTIAN LIFE

F. B. MEYER, D.D.

BAKER BOOK HOUSE
Grand Rapids, Michigan

Reprinted 1978 by
Baker Book House
from the edition issued in 1935
by Marshall, Morgan & Scott Ltd.

ISBN: 0-8010-6054-0

FOREWORD

IN the soul of every man, in which the Holy Spirit has commenced His work, there are depths of yearning desire, which cannot be satisfied from a merely intellectual standpoint. As in David's experience so in ours, both heart and flesh cry out for the living God. But God is *Spirit*, and they that worship Him, or aspire to share in that divine fellowship to which He invites us, must do so in spirit and in truth.

The present decline in church attendance may be largely due to the failure of the pulpit to meet the demand of the human spirit for a more adequate presentation of the spiritual and eternal aspects of our Christian faith, and for a more powerful dynamic and a clearer analysis of the steps that lead through darkness unto God.

For this, there is no need to go beyond the pages of the New Testament. The great saints of the past, whose names shine in the heavenly firmament, found all they needed in the Bible, and what sufficed for them is enough for us. In the following pages those steps are enumerated and explained—however unworthily—that the inquiring soul may be guided in that upward climb and inner experience which culminate in divine likeness.

F. B. MEYER

PRAYER

Lord Jesus, I long to know Thee better, to love Thee more, and to be more absolutely yielded to Thy Spirit. Be my Teacher and Helper, that I may realize Thy Eternal Purpose, and grant me the Holy Spirit in such measure that I may miss nothing that is possible for a redeemed soul. I humbly ask this for Thy Name sake. Amen.

CONTENTS

I. THE "MUST" OF THE NEW BIRTH	9
II. THE "MUST" OF SACRIFICE	21
III. THE "MUST" OF THE DECREASING SELF	35
IV. THE "MUST" OF SERVICE	49
V. THE "MUST" OF SPIRITUAL WORSHIP AND OF THE HOLY SPIRIT	63
VI. THE DAY OF PENTECOST	77
VII. "RECKON ON GOD'S FAITHFULNESS"	93
VIII. FELLOWSHIP WITH CHRIST IN SERVICE	105
IX. OUR KNOWLEDGE OF OUR SAVIOUR	119

THE "MUST" OF THE NEW BIRTH

John iii. 7

SPIRIT = (ETERNAL)
SOUL = (EGO OR SELF)
BODY = (MATERIAL)

WE TOUCH 3 WORLDS	FROM ABOVE
1 Thess. v. 23	DIVINE
Heb. iv. 12	↑
1 Cor. ii. 14	HUMAN
	↑
STUDY A CHILD	ANIMAL
	↑
NECESSITY OF BIRTH	VEGETABLE
John i. 12 and 13	↑
John iii. 7	MINERAL
THE SEED OF BIRTH	THE TEST
1 Pet. i. 23	1 John i. 8–10

NEW BIRTH

"O Heavenly Father! Most glorious and most loving! I thank Thee, that through faith and by the regenerating grace of the Holy Spirit, I have been born from above. Grant me more of the child-spirit, and the simplicity of the child-heart! May Thy Spirit witness with my spirit that I am Thine for ever—through Thy surpassing love!"

I

THE "MUST" OF THE NEW BIRTH

"*Ye must be born from above.*"—JOHN iii. 3, 7

THIS was Christ's opening sentence to Nicodemus, who came to Him under shadow of the night. "*Except a man be born from above* (such is the more accurate rendering of the Greek), *he cannot enter into the kingdom of God . . . Marvel not that I said unto thee . . .*"

But if we are forbidden to marvel at the method, surely we may marvel, first, at the extraordinary opportunity presented to us of becoming the sons and daughters of the Eternal God, and second, that any should treat such an opportunity with neglect.

It is the most marvellous thing in the whole range of human possibility that we mortals should have the offer and opportunity of becoming sons and daughters of the Almighty Eternal God; and if children, then heirs, heirs of God and joint-heirs with Christ. "Beloved, now are we the sons of God, and it doth not yet appear what we shall be!" Yet, it must be so, else the Son of God would never have come to inform us of the wondrous possibilities within our reach. It would be the wonder of eternity if angels were invited to so lofty an honour; but they have never fallen as we have fallen, or sinned as we have sinned. But that we, the children of a fallen race, should have the opportunity of becoming, in the most intimate sense, the sons and daughters of the Lord God Almighty, invited to share His glory—when we quietly consider it—becomes too great a marvel for words!

The wonder becomes even greater whenever we get a glimpse of our own evil hearts! "Surely," says Jonathan Edwards, "it cannot be unreasonable, that, before God delivers us from a state of sin and liability to everlasting woe, He should give us some considerable sense of the evil from which He delivers us, that we may the better appreciate the value of what He is prepared to do for us." And Joseph Alleine tells us that in view of the evil of his own heart, he cried out, "O Lord God, I am lost, and if Thou dost not find out some new way, I shall never be saved. O Lord, have mercy!" And what could be more terrible than the condition of S. H. Hadley, who after his conversion became the rescuer of hundreds in Jerry McAuley's Mission in New York. This is what he says:

"One evening I sat in a saloon in Harlem, a homeless, friendless, dying drunkard. I had pawned or sold everything that could bring drink, and I could not sleep unless I was dead drunk. I had

The "Must" of the New Birth

not eaten for days, and for four nights I had suffered delirium tremens. I had often said, 'I will never be a tramp. I will never be cornered, for when that time comes, if ever it comes, I will find a home in the bottom of the river.'"

Tens of thousands of the lowest and most abandoned have been lifted from the gutter to the throne of the Lamb. They were idolaters, effeminate, adulterers, thieves, covetous, drunkards, revilers, extortioners—but they were washed, sanctified, justified, in the name of Jesus and by the power of the Holy Spirit. "But as many as received Him, to them gave He the right (R.V.) to become the children of God, even to them that believe on His name: which were born, not of blood, nor of the will of the flesh, but of God" (John i. 12, 13).

Our Tripartite Nature

Our chart will help us here. We are capable of touching three levels.

1. *By the spirit* we touch the world above us.

2. *By the soul* we touch the world around us.

3. *By the body* we touch the world below us, the material world, to which our bodies are closely allied by the five gateways of sense—the eye, ear, nose, mouth, and touch.

The soul is the apartment of self-consciousness.

It is the seat of our personality. There our individual character is formed and reigns. God says: "All *souls* are Mine." Along the soul-level lie the faculties of conscience, will, thought, affection, business-faculty—all that contributes to our existence as individual units. From this soul-level is a stairway *upwards to the spirit*, through which we come in touch with God and the spiritual world, and a stairway *down to the body*, by which we come in touch with the world of matter. Alas! that the carpeting on the spiritual stairway is almost as fresh to-day as when first laid down, whilst that on the physical is almost worn to a thread!

Thus man was made in the Image of God (Gen. i. 26).

God is a Trinity in Unity: Father, Son, and Spirit, yet one (2 Cor. xiii. 14).

And each of us is equally a Trinity in Unity: Spirit, Soul, and Body (1 Thess. v. 23).

In the little child, the *body* first appears, then the *soul* awakens to recognize, to express its needs, to cry, to talk, to act. Then, after a while, as the child is taught to close its eyes and pray, a mystic look on the little upturned face reveals its capacity for the unseen, the eternal, and the divine.

It is in the *spirit* that the birth from above takes place. "The Spirit itself beareth witness with our spirit, that we are the children of God" (Rom.

viii. 16). The spirit, also, equally with the body, has its five senses, which come into use when we have been born from above.

It is through the spirit that we come in touch with the Saviour. It is with the spirit we welcome the Lord, who stands and knocks. It is by the spirit that we pray and meditate and grow in grace. It is by the eyes of the heart (another name for the organ of the spirit) that we come to know what is the hope of His calling, the riches of the glory of His inheritance, and the exceeding greatness of His power to usward who believe ! (Eph. i. 18, 19).

The Method of the New Birth

One day as I was walking with a friend in his garden, of which he had every reason to be proud, he said, " This year all my scarlet-runners have failed."

" Why so ! "

" Because there have been so few bees about ; I think that they must have been killed by the hard winter."

Of course I understood what he meant. When bees alight on a flower for the purpose of extracting honey, they, of course, do not realize that they are carrying on their bodies the precious pollen or seed, for which the receptive organ in the flower is waiting. The seed must enter it before fruit can be born, and if there are no bees to carry the seed to the flower, there can be no birth of fruit. Fruit is born from the conjunction of the pollen-seed with the flower that attracts the bee by its beauty or scent.

Similarly the life of God, resident in the Word of God, must be received into our nature, that we may be born from above, not from perishable, but from imperishable seed, through the message of the ever-living God, for all earthly life is as grass. The grass fades and its flower falls, but the Word of the Lord abideth for ever. See 1 Peter i. 23, 24.

It is of the utmost importance, therefore, that we should circulate the Scriptures. They are the divine seed basket! Let children learn them! Let ministers preach them! Let Bible Societies circulate them! The letter of the Word kills, whilst its spirit gives life! " He that soweth the good seed is the Son of Man. The field is the world; and the good seed, these are the sons of the kingdom " (Matt. xiii. 37, 38).

THE HOUR OF THE NEW BIRTH

In many cases—perhaps the majority—God's children are not conscious of the exact hour when they passed from death into life and the great act of regeneration took place. That was the case

The "Must" of the New Birth

with myself. I have no recollection of the time or place, when, as a child, I received into my heart "the incorruptible seed." It may have been, when, as a child, I knelt by my mother's knee to say my evening prayer. In after years, I remember being greatly exercised in my mind by hearing a minister insist that we should know the time and place at which we passed into the family of God. And it was a profound comfort to hear Mr. Spurgeon say: "A man might be sure that he was alive, although he didn't know his birthday."

It may be, that in heaven, some angel will be able to show us, in the Lamb's Book of Life, when, by faith, we passed into the family of God. But in the meanwhile, John, in his first epistle, gives us at least five signs of our having become sons and daughters of the Lord God Almighty:

1. We shall not be recognized by the world (1 John iii. 1).
2. We shall not be able to continue in known sin (1 John iii. 9, 10).
3. We shall cherish a holy love to fellow-members (1 John iii. 14).
4. We shall be conscious of the pulse of God's life and love (1 John v. 1, 2).
5. We shall be kept true and faithful by the Saviour for His work (1 John v. 18, 20).

But the most convincing and helpful sign of all is that supplied in John i. 12, 13: "As many as received Him, to them gave He the right to become the children of God, even to them that believe on His name: which were born, not of blood, nor of the will of the flesh, nor of the will of man, but of God." As the hand outstretched with the back towards heaven and the palm towards earth; so the act by which we become born of the Spirit into the divine family is known in heaven as "birth from above," and on earth as "trusting Jesus"!

THE NEW BIRTH MUST COME FROM ABOVE

The Mineral cannot force its way up into the vegetable kingdom; but the wheat may reach down to incorporate into its texture the metal of the rich soil.

The Vegetable cannot force its way up into the animal kingdom; but as when the cow or horse feeds in the meadow, either can incorporate the grass and lift it into its own organism.

The Animal cannot force its way up into the human, and yet, in the intimacy between its owner and a highly intelligent dog, there may be a kind of uplift into the human level.

So *the Human* cannot force its way into the divine, but, as in the Incarnation, the divine can stoop to our fallen level, uplift and incorporate us, so that we may become partakers of the divine nature, having escaped the corruption, which is in the world, through lust. In addition to this, as we shall see in the next paragraph—" His divine power hath granted unto us all things that pertain unto life and godliness, through the knowledge of Him, who has called us to share in His own glorious character!" See 2 Peter i. 3, 4.

The Inheritance of the Twice-Born

In Luke xv. 31, our Lord once gave His ideal of what is included in the holy relationship into which we enter when we are born into the family of God and become His children through His regenerating grace. " Child, thou art ever with Me, and all that I have is thine." These words contain God's ideal for us all.

(a) *There is Community of Nature.* We become children, not merely by adoption, but by birth, through which we become partakers of the divine nature. Each child of the human race is invited to become a child of God, and He will send forth the Spirit of His Son into the heart, crying, " Abba, Father."

(b) *There is Community of Fellowship.* " Thou art ever with Me." The father in the parable longed for the companionship of these two lads. It may be that their mother had passed away, leaving him desolate, and he thought that in their companionship his loneliness would be relieved. The earthly parent longs as much for the abiding fellowship of his children as God does for ours. He goes far, when He says, "Son, give Me thine heart," but no words can exaggerate the yearning of infinite love for the close fellowship of those for whom He spared not His own Son.

(c) *There is Community of Possession.* "All that I have is thine." We are called to be sons; and if sons, "then heirs, heirs of God and joint-heirs with Christ." It is incredible, but it is true! Just now, we are in our minority, and are not entrusted with our full property. We are under stewards and guardians until the time appointed by our Father; but it is certain that we are not bond-servants, but sons, and if sons, then heirs of God. All things are ours, whether life or death, things present or things to come, and, best of all, the unsearchable riches of Christ.

Oh, soul of man or woman, I pray thee never to rest till, by simple faith in the Saviour, thou becomest a child and enterest upon thine inexhaustible heritage!

Spirit of Childhood! Loved of God,
By Jesu's Spirit now bestow'd;
How often have I longed for Thee;
O Jesus, form Thyself in me!

And help me to become a child
While yet on earth, meek, undefiled,
That I may find Thee always near,
And Paradise around me here.
                    GERHARDT TERSTEEGEN

THE "MUST" OF SACRIFICE

John iii. 14

The SPIRIT
The SOUL or I
The BODY

THE OBJECTIVE ASPECT OF THE CROSS	THE SUBJECTIVE ASPECT OF THE CROSS
The Message to the Greeks. John xii. 26	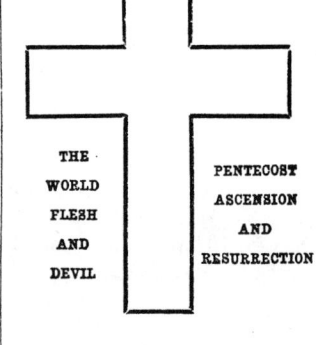
Christ died for—	
1. The World's Sin. John i. 29	
2. To Bruise the Serpent. Heb. ii. 14	
3. To Obtain the Keys. Rev. i. 18	
4. For the Separation of the Church. 2 Cor. v. 14, 15	
5. For our Sanctification. 1 Pet. ii. 24	Gal. ii. 20, v. 24, vi. 14; Rom. vi. 11

SACRIFICE

"*Most Holy God, how can I ever thank Thee enough that Thou didst not spare Thyself, when Thy Son, our Saviour, died to save us! I thank Thee that He loved me, and gave Himself for me, and that His death has opened to me, and all who believe, the gates of eternal life.*"

II

THE " MUST " OF SACRIFICE

" The Son of Man must be lifted up."—JOHN iii. 14

THE most wonderful thing that we know of God is not His omnipotence, omniscience, or omnipresence, but that He was willing, in the person of Jesus Christ, to undergo the infinite sacrifice of Calvary. He is described as the Blessed or Happy God ; and He is that, not because of His resources, but because, though He was rich, yet in the person of Christ He became poor, that through His poverty we might become rich. This is acknowledged by the heavenly hosts as they cry : " Worthy is the Lamb that was slain to receive power, and riches, and wisdom, and might, and honour, and glory, and blessing."

Self-sacrifice is rightly recognized as the supreme trait of a noble character. Take, for instance, the spirit of Abraham Lincoln's address to his friends and neighbours, as he left home to become the President of the United States :

" My friends, no one, not in my situation, can appreciate the feelings of sadness that come over me at this parting. To you and to the kindness of this people I owe everything. Here I have lived for a quarter of a century, and have passed from a young to an old man. I now leave you—not knowing when or whether I shall ever return—with a task before me greater than that which rested upon Washington. Without the aid of that Divine Being who ever attended him, I cannot succeed. With His assistance, I cannot fail. Trusting in Him, who can go with *me* and remain with *you*, let us confidently hope ' that all may yet be well.' To His care commending you, as I hope in your prayers you will commend me, I bid you an affectionate farewell."

As he was about to choose his cabinet, he said: " We have a great task on our hands, and it seems the heaviest load has fallen on my poor shoulders. We must save this Union, not only for ourselves and our children, but for the world. I must get the best men that I can to help me. If . . . can help to save this Union, it does not matter how he treats me."

Nobler words than those have seldom been uttered; and when he had finished the task that was allotted to him, he was cut down by the assassin; but yet even this heroic life pales in glory, when we see Jesus facing Calvary.

He knew He would tread the winepress alone!

He knew that though He loved the race, and

The "Must" of Sacrifice 23

desired to save every item of it, that the majority would repudiate Him.

He knew that He would stand before unfallen worlds and ranks of beings, as identified with a world's sin.

He knew that His Father's face would be hidden, as by an eclipse.

He knew that the conflict would break His heart and force the sweat of blood out on His forehead.

He knew that the Serpent of hell would bruise His heel, and that He would appear as a Lamb that had been slain.

He knew that those whom He had chosen out of the world would deny Him and flee.

Yet—He slackened not His pace, but laying aside the insignia of His glory, He became obedient unto death, even the death of the Cross!

Looking at this stupendous act, shall we not catch the infection of His self-giving? Shall we not follow Him so far as we can? "Christ," says the apostle, "has left us an example that we should follow His steps." It is not what we get, but what we give; not our own pleasure, but the uplift of the fallen, and the extrication of those who are slipping into the pit; not ridding ourselves of burdens, but bearing the burden of others. This is the path of true blessedness, the path trodden by all saints, the path which led Christ to Gethsemane and

Calvary, but has ended in the throne! Follow that path, and life will become transcendently useful and blessed!

But there is an infinite chasm between our highest attainments and the divine self-giving of our Saviour to redeem and save us. He trod that winepress alone, and of all the people there were none with Him! So far as we know, Gethsemane and Calvary have no equivalents throughout God's universe. They are the wonder into which angels desire to look, and the theme of the untiring song of the redeemed.

THE WONDER OF THE CROSS!

How can mortal man tell out all the height and depth, the length and breadth—of the infinite self-giving of our Lord?

(a) *The Lord Jesus died for the sin of the race.* "Behold," said the Baptist, "the Lamb of God, that taketh away the sin of the world." He, the sinless One, who lived in the eternal sphere of holiness and peace, moved by love, voluntarily assumed connection with the fallen race of man, and undertook by identification with us to bear our just penalty and doom. Here was His greatest greatness. Not that He had ever dwelt in the bosom of the Father. Not that He had ever been the channel and organ through which the will of the Creator flowed and worlds came into being. Not that He was the heir of all things. But that He stooped to take our fallen nature upon Himself. George Herbert said that when He laid down His crown it became the Milky Way: that when He laid aside His robes, they became the sunset clouds. Finally, as the sinless second Adam, He gathered to Himself the sin of the race, and bore it to Calvary. He became the propitiatory sacrifice for us all. He voluntarily laid down His life to become our ransom price. He had power to lay it down and power to take it up again, and He laid it down to obtain our full salvation. He, who knew no sin, by His own act was made sin for us that we might become the righteousness of God. Do not neglect this great act of love for thee and the world! Trust thyself with the all-loving One!

Before us all lie the possibility and peril of contracting-out from our share in the finished work of Calvary. The man in the parable who had been entrusted with ten thousand talents, and who passed his poor debtor into prison till he paid a hundred pence, was rightly punished for that act. He had forfeited his Lord's forgiveness, and was recommitted to the torment of the prison! But the man "who married a wife" was equally excluded from the great supper! Do not be content to hear or read about the mystery of the divine self-giving! Accept your share in it and be thankful; and then unite yourself with the love of God and become a channel through which He may pour it forth upon the world. When once a man understands the meaning of Calvary and not only accepts it for himself, but unites himself with it, he enters upon an absolutely new zone or sphere of living. Old things pass away! All things become new! The love of Christ constrains him, no longer to live to himself, but to Him who loved him and gave Himself for him.

Stand once more before the Cross! Forget all else, except that thou and Christ are there alone! Say aloud, " He bore *my* sins in His own body on the Tree," and add, " I also am crucified with Him. I have no other aim in life than to unite myself with His death, that I may share His life. Henceforth I desire to live by daily, hourly faith in the Son of God, who loved *me* and gave Himself for *me*!"

(b) *When He died, the Lord Jesus bruised the Serpent's head and broke his power for ever.* Probably there are *hosts of demons*, but there is *only one devil*. He is the prince of the power of the air. It is absurd and wrong to speak lightly of him. By those who are out of Christ, he is greatly to be feared. Our Lord spoke of him as " the Prince of this world," and Paul refers to him as "the god of this world." The Saviour encountered him on the threshold of His public ministry, and in the wilderness it was settled that He would hold His supremacy, not as the vicegerent of Satan, but by the victory of the Cross. In the garden, He stood for the race as its second Adam; and we dare not imagine what would have been the fate of humanity or of the universe, if our Saviour had collapsed through mortal weakness in Gethsemane. He came very near collapsing as He lifted the cup—which might not pass from Him—to His lips. The peril was imminent—for we are told in Hebrews v. 7 that, in the days of His flesh, He offered up prayers and supplications unto Him *who was able to save Him from death*—and this surely implies that there was fear, lest in the extremity of that final conflict His body would collapse. It was the hour of the power of darkness! His failure, then, would have changed the destiny of our race, and shrouded the heavens with the blackness of despair. How little do the frivolous children of this world recognize their indebtedness to the Christ, whom they ignore! But, thanks to the angel that stood beside and strengthened Him, our Saviour destroyed him that had the power of death, the devil, and delivered those who, through fear of death, were all their lifetime subject to bondage. As we stand in our risen and ascended Lord, we see Satan fall as lightning from heaven. He gives us authority to tread on all the power of the enemy. As a man in uniform is able to regulate the traffic of a crowded street, because he represents the authority of the State, so the weakest child of God, who stands in the victory of Calvary, is able to resist and overcome all the power of the evil spirits that infect the air. If you can only claim to be in the *feet* of the mystical body of the risen Lord, you can tread on serpents and scorpions and on all the power of the devil.

(c) *Our Saviour, when dying, not only put away sin by the sacrifice of Himself, but He opened doors that none can shut and shut doors that none can open.* His death was a voluntary act of love. He said, "No man taketh My life from Me, I lay it down of Myself; I have power to lay it down and I have power to take it again. This command I received of My Father." He wrested the keys of death from the hand of Satan, and they now hang at His girdle. Hades is the ante-chamber of paradise. John heard Him say, "I am He that liveth. I became dead, and behold, I am alive for evermore, and I have the keys of Death and Hades."

Clearly, then, our Lord commands the door that opens on eternity. When we come to the end of this valley of shadow, we shall find Him waiting for us with a smile. Stephen saw Him standing there; and, as the first-born from among the dead, Jesus welcomed the first Christian martyr to his crown. How good it will be to see Him and hear Him bid us enter into His joy! The grave shall have no terrors, neither death its sting. As a little babe is welcomed into the world with a kiss and finds gentle arms waiting to cradle it, and many good things prepared for it, so, when we open our eyes on that new world, we shall hear His voice, musical as many waters, and see His face, once wet with tears, but then radiant with eternal dawn.

(d) *The Cross also stands for separation.* It is not enough to reach out our hands to receive the blessings that Christ has won for us. We must live as those who are identified with Him.

> "One when He died; One when He rose!
> One when He triumphed o'er our foes!
> One when in heaven He took His seat!
> And heaven rejoiced o'er hell's defeat."

The whole New Testament rings with this thought, as in Romans vi. 5–11; Colossians ii. 20, iii. 1–4; and Ephesians iv. 17–24.

Yield yourselves to God as those who have risen from the dead, and surrender your faculties to God to be used by Him as weapons to maintain the right! You have become one with Jesus in sharing the benefits of His death, now partake of and manifest His risen life! He is the vine, be you the branches! Our old self was crucified with Christ, so that we should no longer be the slaves of sin; but as we shared Christ's death, we should also share His life! Reckon yourselves, therefore, as dead to sin, but as living to God, through union with the risen Saviour! Let His Cross be the barrier between your former life and your present!

This will greatly help us to decide doubtful matters! We have, of course, to mix with men, to conduct our business, to take our place in the life around; but our behaviour must be guided by the principles which emanate from our risen and ascended Lord. As laid down by the Master in the Sermon on the Mount, they must become our guiding stars. We shall find all these things to be possible, through the Holy Spirit's gracious help.

A young girl who had become a true disciple of Christ, had partaken of the Holy Communion, and was teaching in our Sunday school, brought me an invitation that had been sent to her, to join a very worldly set in an evening of frivolous amusement. Now, I heartily believe in all *natural* recreation and pleasure. High spirits! Bright faces! Dexterity in games! These, so far as my judgment goes, are perfectly consistent with a healthy Christian life. They must not be an end in themselves; but they help to maintain a healthy mind in a healthy body. But, in the case before us, those conditions were absent. This young girl would be tempted in her dress, and in conforming to certain phases of the modern dance, to overstep the limit which divides God's children from the fashion of this world. I did not desire to settle the matter for her; but resolved to teach her how to determine such questions for herself. I, therefore, drew on paper the picture of the Cross. On the *left* side I inserted the words—" The World, the Flesh, the Devil." On the *right* side the words—" Resurrection, Ascension, Second Advent."

" Where shall I write: 'Fancy Dress Ball'? Shall I write it here on the right-hand side ? "

" No, *it will not do there.*"

Then I proposed to put it beside the Crown of Thorns.

" No, *it will not do there.*"

Then I wrote it at the foot, by the Grave of Christ, through which she had passed in her baptism.

" No, *it will not do there.*"

Finally, after a pause, she consented to my writing the words on the left hand of the Cross, next to the World, which is still under the dominion of the Flesh and the Devil. She saw the incongruity of that kind of amusement with her profession of Christ, and caught sight of a principle which will guide her in all similar positions.

Let it never be said or thought, that the life

hidden with Christ in God is sad or sour! He, who created the song of the singing-bird, the infectious laughter of the child, the dancing sunlight of the woodland, and loved to see the children playing in the market-place, has not brought melancholy into the world. When He came to the wedding feast, He gave the best wine last. His religion can never be counted a kill-joy.

For the most part, the redeemed soul loses its taste for the things that once charmed and engrossed it.

A young working girl, speaking of a certain form of amusement, once said to me: "I went every evening, as soon as I got home from work. I thought I couldn't live without it; but when I found Jesus, and Jesus found me, I lost all my taste for it. I went the other night to see what it was that had held me, but I came out in ten minutes, and shall never go back again." Surely the Scripture tells truly that, in Christ, old things pass away, and lo, all things become new!

Let us never forget those words of Hartley Coleridge! It is a fitting epitaph on the sacrifice of Calvary, when its spirit has entered a human life.

> "Think not the faith by which the just shall live
>   Is a dead creed, a map correct of heaven,
> Far less a feeling fond and fugitive,
>   A thoughtless gift, withdrawn as soon as given;
> It is an affirmation and an act
> Which makes eternal truth be present fact!"

Yes, *for Thy sake*, O God Most High!
O Man Most Meek! we too can die—
Die to the death which Thou hast slain,
Die to the deepest source of pain,
And walk, by Love's sustaining store,
As seekers of our own no more.

We can hear more than ear hath heard,
Life of the World! in this Thy Word;
And wastes shall break forth into song,
As in its power we pass along;
For lo! in hidden deep accord,
The servant *may be* like his Lord,
And *Thy* love, our love shining through,
May tell the world that Thou art true,
Till those who see us see Thee too.

A. L. Waring

THE "MUST" OF SELFLESSNESS

John iii. 30, 34

SPIRIT—GOD CONSCIOUSNESS

SOUL—SELF CONSCIOUSNESS
(Flesh—Rom. vii. 18)

BODY—WORLD CONSCIOUSNESS

The Self-Life gives its BIAS TO THE PROPERTIES OF THE SOUL	THE NOT-I of the Christ-Life
THE DIVINE VERDICT Jer. xvii. 7–11 Matt. xv. 19, 20 Gal. v. 17–21 THE APOSTLE'S OUTCRY Rom. vii. 7–25	1. Reckon Death. Rom. vi. 11, viii. 1–4 2. The Help of the Holy Spirit. John xiv. 16 Rom. viii. 2 3. The Love of Christ. 2 Cor. v. 14

SELF-CONCERN

"*Lord Jesus! I humbly pray that the Holy Spirit may lead me to understand and experience the inner meaning of Calvary! May I also die to sin and live unto righteousness! One with Thee in Thy death, may I be one with Thee in Thy eternal victory, over the world, the flesh, and the devil! Make me more than a conqueror, through Thy blood!*"

III

THE "MUST" OF THE DECREASING SELF

WHEN our sins have been forgiven through the sacrifice of our Lord, there is still to be considered the problem of the holy life; but this can only be satisfactorily settled by the deep teaching of the New Testament.

Three solutions have been proposed, though only the last named will satisfy.

THE PAGAN SOLUTION

This method characterized the great philosophy of the Greek world led by Plato, Socrates, and Aristotle. Their one thought was for the soul of man to lift itself by its own effort; and they placed before it the ideal of *Beauty* as its prime incentive. Paul, however, who had been brought up under that system, confessed sadly, "The good I would, I do not; the evil, that I would not, I do." The Greek love of beauty remains to-day in the buildings, statues, and literature which have come down to us. Profound thinkers embodied their ideals in this manner, but their disciples failed to realize their spiritual and moral conceptions, though they were enamoured of their ideals.

The Greek philosophy therefore ended in despair. The Fall of Troy; the wanderings of Ulysses; Tantalus always missing the tantalizing water; Sisyphus rolling the stone uphill, which always returned on him; Laocoon and his sons, entangled by the serpents; Prometheus, devoured by the vulture; and Hercules, with his arduous labours—all tell the same tale of inability to realize their ideals. All confess with Paul—who had been educated in the great university of Tarsus, where these ideals were taught—that the world by wisdom knew not God; and that it remained for the foolishness of preaching—foolish according to the philosophy of the age—to save those who longed to realize their ideals.

The Baptist's Solution

There are few stories more instructive. His parents apparently died in his early life, and he was led by the Spirit into the wild mountains that stretched across to the Jordan. There he lived with God on the simplest fare and wrapped in the atmosphere of the unseen and eternal. One day, as a caravan of pilgrims was approaching the Holy City, he met and accosted them by the challenge:

The "Must" of the Decreasing Self

"Repent, for the kingdom of heaven is at hand! Make ready the way of the Lord! Make His paths straight!" The startled pilgrims had a strange story to tell when they reached Jerusalem. The tidings spread like fire from lip to lip, that God had visited His people, that Elijah had again appeared; and there went out to him Jerusalem and all Judea. In fact, the whole land awoke to a new voice, which may be regarded as epitomizing and uttering the great moral code of the Old Testament.

That noble system, God-given and God-inspired, was a stepping-stone to Christ, but it failed to satisfy those who came under its influence. There was a lack which John the Baptist confessed! He could administer the outward rite of baptism, but could not impart salvation. He could only prepare the way for the Coming One, and eagerly wait for the manifestation of the Christ. As the morning star, he was bound to decrease! He could not give power unto salvation! But he uttered the cry of the heart in its penitence and eager yearning for a mightier spiritual dynamic than that which up to then had prevailed. Therefore, the multitudes of earnest seekers ebbed away from him to Jesus Christ, and only a comparative few remained to listen to the herald's voice. This was resented by his immediate followers, but he rebuked them. He was only the bridegroom's friend and forerunner! The bride was not his! It was his joy to hear the bridegroom's voice! He was content that his own popularity should wane, whilst Christ's must increase with ever-growing power!

The failure of the system taught by John the Baptist (which indeed embodied the teaching of the moral law) consisted in the difficulty of mastering the self-life, which the apostle refers to as "the flesh." The flesh, therefore, is the bias which continually asserts itself. It is the tendency, of which we are all conscious, which, with strange persistence, determines our thought and action towards self-aggrandizement. If we drop the "h" and spell "flesh" backwards, it comes out as s-e-l-f, which follows us like a shadow and is the curse of our inward life. We become sick and tired of its constant intrusion, its haunting criticism about others, its inevitable commentary on whatever we do or say. The apostle was very sensitive to this constant assertion of this self-life; and he cried out, "Oh, wretched man that I am! who shall deliver me?" It seemed as though, as in the awful Roman punishment, he was bound to the decaying body of a dead criminal. "Who shall deliver me from this body of death?" Obviously, therefore, it was necessary in the process of time for the Divine Spirit to reveal a method of holiness which should do for mankind what the philosophy of Greece, and even the lofty

Mosaic system as represented by John the Baptist, had failed to realize.

THE SOLUTION OF THE NEW TESTAMENT

(a) *We must reckon ourselves dead to sin.* We have already seen that the self-life is our greatest struggle. It is so sensitive, so hungry for prominence and praise, so eager! In speaking thus, we must, of course, distinguish between our natural endowments, which are sacred gifts, for which we may thank God, and our desire to exploit them to obtain admiration and praise from our associates. As we have seen, it is the ego-bias which hurts all and spoils the music of our lives! We are tempted to be proud of our humility! When singing God's praise, we are apt to be proud of our voice! The minister is tempted to feel pride over his sermon on " Humility "!

We must give this ubiquitous self no quarter; but the conflict, as Paul explains in Romans vii., will be long and arduous. As the sun rises, its beams strike lower and yet lower down the pit. We find depths of self-ness, ever lower down, affecting the motives of our life. Often shall we repeat the apostle's cry for deliverance; and there *is* deliverance in our daily dying to the self-life by our union with the Cross of Christ.

Our old man, that is, our self-life, has been nailed to the Saviour's Cross. Through our union with our Lord in His death, we, in the purpose of God, have died to sin even as He died to it. We were one with Him in His grave and we are one with Him in His resurrection. That is our position, objectively; but by faith we must make it subjectively real. We must consider that our old self was crucified with Christ and that in the Cross we have passed into the glorious liberty of His resurrection. The death that Jesus died was a death to sin once for all; and the life that He lives, He lives to God. So we must regard ourselves as dead to sin and self, but as living to God through our union with our Saviour. *The self-life may not be dead, but we are dead to it!*

One summer afternoon, when I reached the great Auditorium at Northfield, I found Mr. Moody and his brother on the platform, and between them a young apple-tree just dug up and brought from the neighbouring orchard. There were about eight hundred or a thousand people in the audience When I reached the platform the following dialogue took place:

Mr. Moody to his brother: "What have you here?"

"An apple-tree."

"Was it always an apple-tree?"

The "Must" of the Decreasing Self 41

"Oh no, it was a forest-sapling, but we have inserted an apple-graft."

Mr. Moody to me: "What does that make you think of?"

"You and I were forest-saplings, with no hope of bearing fruit, but the Jesus-nature has been grafted into us by the Holy Spirit."

To his brother: "Does the forest-sapling give you trouble?"

"Why, yes, it is always sending out shoots under the graft, and they drain off the sap."

"What do you do with them?"

"We pinch them off with finger and thumb, but they are always coming out, lower down the tree."

Then he turned to me, and asked if there was anything like it in the life of the *Spirit*; to which I replied: "It is a parable of our experience. The old self-life is always sending out its shoots, but we must be merciless to them. In our earlier stages we deal with the more superficial appeals of the self-life to our vanity and the like. But as we grow older we become aware of their presence always lower down."

A further illustration may be given from the experience of Dr. Tauler of Strasburg, who did much to prepare the way for Luther and the Reformation. He was a fine preacher, and the whole city hung upon his lips. He was greatly startled, therefore, when a humble Switzer, one of the Society of "the

Friends of God," named Nicholas of Basle, crossed the mountains, entered his church, and said, " You must die, Dr. Tauler! Before you can do your greatest work for God, the world, and this city, you must die to yourself, your gifts, your popularity, and even your own goodness, and when you have learned the full meaning of the Cross you will have new power with God and man."

At first he greatly resented this intrusion, but ultimately left his pulpit for a time, and retired for meditation, prayer, and heart-searching. As the inner vision grew clearer, he came to realize how much of his ministry had been inspired by the inveterate wish to make an impression, not simply for Christ's sake, but with the view of maintaining and increasing his own prestige. Finally he left " life's glory dead " at the foot of the Cross, and resolved to have one objective, and one only, Jesus Christ and Him crucified. From that moment his preaching began to help people as never before, and prepared for Luther and the new Age.

This story might be indefinitely repeated. Some of us can never forget the hymn composed by the late Pastor Theodore Monod of Paris in his first radiant vision of a life hidden in Christ with God:

> " All of Self and none of Thee!
> Some of Self and some of Thee!
> Less of Self and more of Thee!
> None of Self and all of Thee!"

The "Must" of the Decreasing Self 43

"*Reckon yourselves to be dead indeed unto sin, but alive unto God, through Jesus Christ our Lord.*"

(b) *We must receive more of the grace of the Holy Spirit.* In Romans vii., the apostle complains of being tied and bound by the self-life. He is like a caged bird, which beats its breast against the bars of its cage, in vain aspirations for liberty. Then, suddenly, in Romans viii., he changes his note and cries, "There is now no more of this self-condemnation for those who are in Christ Jesus, who walk and live after the Spirit, because the law of the Spirit of life, in Christ Jesus, has made them free from the law of sin and death."

Let us stand together on the deck of an ocean-bound steamer and watch the flight of a sea-gull. There is, of course, the downward pull of gravitation; but, for every pull downward, there is a stroke of the live bird's wing on the elastic air; and this more than compensates for the downward pull. That stroke, we know, is due to the spirit of life, which throbs in the bird's breast. So, by the Holy Spirit, who indwells our spirit, there is given to each one of us the very life of our glorious Saviour. The regularity, immediacy, and quality of the Christ-life are more than sufficient to counteract the down-pull of sin. At the first slight suggestion of sin, the Holy Spirit resists the self-life, so that we may not do the things that we otherwise would; nor shall we fall into those sins of will and thought and act, which were once natural to us. "If we live by the Spirit, by the Spirit let us walk." See Galatians v. 16-26. The Spirit will lust against the flesh and obtain absolute victory which will fill our hearts with joy. Indeed, temptation may even promote a stronger character by making Jesus a more living reality.

Some years ago a number of Christian men, of whom I am thankful to have been one, were spending an autumn evening around the fire in the study of the late Canon Wilberforce. We were discussing the problem of the inner life. After one or two had laid stress on negativing temptation, an elderly clergyman stood up and said:

"I am naturally of a very irascible temper. When addressing the children of my Sunday school recently, they were more than usually restless. I was on the point of losing my temper, but was led to look up, and I saw the Saviour standing there, so calm, and sweet, and strong that I felt led to say, 'Lord, give me Thy patience, for mine is giving out.' At once, He seemed to drop into my heart a lump of His own patience, and I could have stood twice as many children, and twice as much inattention, without losing myself. From that moment, I have followed the same method. When tempted to pride, I have said, 'Thy humility,

Lord.' In temptations to quick temper, I have said, ' Thy patience, Lord.' Thus temptation has become to me a positive means of grace."

There our conversation stopped. Nothing better could be said. When we met next morning, Wilberforce and I confessed that the old clergyman's experience should henceforth be our own, and that we would take advantage of temptation for the fresh claiming of the life of our risen Lord ! Thus the Spirit of life in Christ Jesus would make us more than conquerors, because each temptation would prompt us to obtain fresh supplies through the Holy Spirit.

(c) *We must make more and more of the personal love between the Lord Jesus and ourselves.* " We are married to Another, even to Him that was raised from the dead." When a woman has obtained a divorce from her husband on account of his cruelty and infidelity, and has become the wife of a man of noble and pure character, she has no taste to return to her former husband, and she does not fear him. Her heart and life are so entirely satisfied, that if she encounters him in the street, she may shudder, but she knows that she is safe. If he dares to approach her, she clings closer to the man of her choice. So, the apostle says, we are married to Another, even to Him that arose from the dead, the Lover and Saviour of men, and we cling closer to Him, whenever the old, evil self-life appears.

When the wife of Tigranes came out of the pavilion of Alexander the Great, they asked her what she thought of the costly adorning and furniture of the interior, and she replied that she had no eyes, except for the man—her husband—who had willingly offered to die if she might be spared. Oh, that we knew more of that kind of love! So that the least suggestion of self-ness, of self-aggrandizement, of self-pride or self-pity might be wiped out before our love for Jesus. May that love be shed abroad in our hearts, so that Jesus, Jesus only, and Jesus always, may be our supreme passion!

When Ulysses passed the Siren Sisters, whose enticing songs tempted mariners to the cruel rocks, he tied his sailors and rowers to their seats; but when Orpheus made the same voyage, he had no need of ropes and bands, because his music was sweeter than theirs.

I heard of a young girl, a student in the Edinburgh University, who loudly declared her dislike of mathematics; but her whole attitude was reversed when she was loved by and loved the finest mathematician in the university.

So may the love of Christ bind us to Him, and may love take up the harp of life and smite on all

The "Must" of the Decreasing Self 47

its cords with might, smite the cord of self, so that it may pass in trembling out of sight!

"The love of Christ constraineth us, that we should no longer live unto ourselves, but unto Him that loved us and gave Himself for us." That is the secret of a holy life!

It is good to reckon ourselves dead to sin.

It is good to draw constantly on the resources of our Saviour.

But it is best, when we are lost in the overmastering love of Jesus.

It was said of Count Zinzendorf, the friend of the Moravians, that he had one passion, and one passion only—" the love of Christ "!

So, through the thunder comes a human voice
Saying, "O heart I made, a heart beats here!
Face, My hands fashioned, see it in Myself!
Thou hast no power nor mayst conceive of Mine,
But love I gave thee, with Myself to love,
And thou must love Me, who have died for thee."
ROBERT BROWNING

THE "MUST" OF SERVICE
John iv. 4

SPIRIT—GOD'S PLAN
SOUL—MYSELF—OUR PLAN
BODY—SENSES' PLAN

THE HEAVENLY PURPOSE	THE EARTHLY FULFILMENT
Tabernacle— Heb. viii. 5	John iv. 4–42
The PATTERN of our Lord's Life { John v. 19, 30 / John x. 18 / John xii. 49 / John xv. 10 }	UNFOLDING THE PLAN { Time iv. 6 / Agent iv. 10 / Stages iv. 19, 26, 28, 42 }
Jeremiah— Jer. i. 5–19 / Philip— Acts viii. 26–40 / Cornelius— Acts x. 3–48 / Paul— Acts xvi. 7–40	THE ULTIMATE RESULTS { The Father / Christ / The Spirit / Worship / Ministry }

SERVICE

"Most gracious God! Teach me to do Thy will. Make Thy way clear and plain before my face! Help me to run with patience along the path that Thou hast marked out for me, to build on Thy pattern, and in all things to glorify Thee on the earth, regardless of all consequences to myself."

IV

THE "MUST" OF SERVICE

"And He must needs go through Samaria."—JOHN IV. 4

GOD is prepared to undertake the direction of every human life which is placed at His disposal. The question of guidance is therefore of imperative importance for each living soul, as it passes out into this mortal life. Since God says, "All souls are mine," He must have, therefore, a distinct purpose for each, and sends each out with resources within reach sufficient to supply all its need, according to His riches in Christ Jesus. It may even be that before the soul joins the body, it stands before its Maker to receive its directory or charge. Our Lord at least said, "To this end have I been born, and to this end am I come into the world" (John xviii. 37). At the close of our earth-life we shall again stand before the judgment seat of Christ to give an account of the things done in the body, whether good or bad (2 Cor. v. 10).

The Greek word in Ephesians ii. 10, translated *workmanship*, might be transferred bodily into our language as *poem*. We might therefore read the verse thus—" We are His poem, created in Christ

Jesus unto good works, which God hath before prepared that we should walk in them." Nothing can give us more confidence as we look out on our life than that God is not only prepared to unfold His programme for us, but is also prepared "to make all grace abound towards us, that we, having all sufficiency in all things, may abound to every good work" (2 Cor. ix. 8). He will not only supply seed to the sower, but will also be responsible for his food! Thus our lives will become enriched to all liberality, which shall elicit from many hearts thanksgiving to God.

One Saturday afternoon, Dr. Gunsaulus of Chicago was preparing for his sermon on the following day. While thus engaged, his nephew, a flippant, careless fellow, rather lightly asked him the topic on which he was preparing to preach. He learned that it was on those words of our Lord, "To this end was I born, and for this cause came I into the world."

Rather jauntily he said, "What do you think I was born for?"

His uncle replied, "I don't know," and his nephew answered, "Neither do I."

As he went along the street, he came to a theatre which had caught fire, while crowded with people, and many were being crushed and trampled to death by the mad rush for the door. The young fellow at once threw off his coat, and began dragging out body after body of these people, some dead and others dying, till he was stricken by a burning timber, knocked almost senseless, and carried to the nearest hospital.

Dr. Gunsaulus reached his bedside just in time to hear him say, "Uncle, for this cause I was born, and for this I was sent into the world, that I might save those ten people."

There was a tragedy there, that none of us ever wish to meet. But what a comfort it will be at last, to feel that we have glorified Christ's name and have finished the work which He gave us to do.

THE SAMARITAN ROUTE

It is said of our Lord that He "must needs go through Samaria." Owing to the bad feeling between the Samaritans and the Galilean Jews, it was their habit to take the circuitous route on the eastern bank of the Jordan instead of the direct route through Samaritan territory. In this case, there was a "needs be," and an imperative reason, for Christ to take the latter route. This dependence on the Father for guidance is constantly referred to in the Gospels. See John v. 19, x. 18, xii. 49, xv. 10. It was thus consistent with His constant attitude to the Father during His earthly life. He was, of course, One with the Father and the Holy Spirit in the Holy Trinity, but He refused to avail Himself of His divine prerogatives, that He might be the Author and Finisher of the faith-life, and be able to help us, as He could not have done, unless He had borne our griefs and carried our sorrows. It was as if a father, who desired to encourage his son, whose right arm had been amputated, forwent the use of his own right hand, which he carried permanently bound behind his back, and therefore could sympathize with and help the lad, because he was suffering from the same limitations—though in *his* case they had been voluntarily assumed, and might, at any moment, be laid aside.

In the East, and especially in the olden times, a servant never received the word of command from master or mistress, but watched carefully the movement of their hands. So the eyes of the slave were always, as the Psalmist puts it, "unto the hand" of master or mistress (Ps. cxxiii. 2). It was probably with reference to this that our Saviour said, "The Son can do nothing of Himself, but what He *seeth* the Father doing" (John v. 19). There are three possible plannings for human life. We may be guided by our senses—"We like this, or do not like that." We may be guided by our own will and choice. But, best of all, we may be guided, as our Lord was, by constantly waiting for the indication of God's purpose, which indication is like a deep-toned bell ringing in our heart-depths, but finally corroborated by circumstances and certainly vindicated by results.

When God gives the Pattern, He will provide the Material

One Sunday morning, I was sitting on the porch of Mr. Moody's home, looking down on the Connecticut River. We were talking of the ways of God, and he recalled a sermon of Dr. Andrew Bonar on the words, repeated five times in Scripture, See that thou make all things according to the pattern shown thee on the Mount." Dr. Bonar described the tabernacle pattern as woven out of sunbeams; and Moses walked with God from one part to another of the ethereal structure, learning the specific reason for each. When, for instance, they viewed the altar of sacrifice, God explained that in process of time Calvary would bear the weight of the dying Saviour; and, as they looked on the laver, God would explain that the soul, redeemed by the blood of Christ, would always need cleansing. So also the significance of the altar of incense, the veil, the ark, and the mercy-seat. When presently Moses returned to the people, he discovered that for everything which had been revealed in the vision, there was exact and adequate provision in the gifts of the people. This is a most helpful lesson. The first thing for any of us is not to run hither and thither, consulting people or soliciting their help, but to be perfectly assured that we are in the mind of the Lord, and that He will supply all our need, according to His riches in glory by Christ Jesus. It must never be forgotten that none of those that live in God's purposes need ever be ashamed. His delays are not denials. "From of old, men have not heard, nor perceived by the ear, neither hath eye seen, O God, beside Thee, what He hath prepared for him that waiteth for Him" (Isa. lxiv. 4, 5).

The Reason for Our Lord's Imperative Journey

All had been carefully arranged. When a woman awoke that morning in the little town of Sychar that lay in the lap of the twin mountains of Ebal and Gerizim, she little realized that that day would revolutionize, not only her own life, but the lives of her people and of untold thousands beside. Through the happenings of those hours, her story would become embalmed in the history of the race, and she, as tradition says, would take her first steps on a path that ended in her martyrdom.

The "Must" of Service 55

Her nature was passionate and intense. She was sick and weary, because she had sought to satisfy its demands with illicit love. Man after man had deceived her. Already five husbands had come and gone, and she was at this time living with another. She had almost ceased to believe in love of any kind. The spring-tide of her life had already faded into autumn with its sere and yellow leaf. How little she realized the possibilities that only awaited the touch of Christ to elicit their rich and full service to the world! Her sister-women would not brook her presence at the well that was situated at the bottom of the declivity, where the ancient road travelled from South to North. Her life had become so notorious that she had no alternative than to carry her pitcher to the well in the sultry noon, instead of waiting for the cool of the evening, as the others did.

She was not destitute of religion. She believed that Jacob lived in sight of those mountains, and had drunk water from that well. She believed in the God of Abraham, Isaac, and Jacob; and did not suppose that there could be any advance on that old-world religion. She had heard many discussions as to the rival claims of the temples at Jerusalem and Gerizim, and accepted the arguments in support of the latter. Like many others, she believed that some day the long-looked-for Messiah would come and explain all things. In the meanwhile, she was weary and out of heart. Her lonely midday visit to that well seemed to epitomize her inner experience of heart-sickness. *Religion appeared to her like letting a pitcher down into a pit or well, but the water was soon exhausted. It had to be replenished again and again.*

Such were some of the thoughts that occupied her mind. Here was a woman of great capacity for good or evil. One that could bring a whole city-full to the feet of God! A heart that could vibrate to the touch of pure and holy love, as she had yielded it to evil! Was it not wonderful that Jesus must needs pass through Samaria! And His arrival was so timed that the apostles would be absent, seeking their midday meal; and thus the conversation between herself and Christ could not be overheard or scrutinized! Was not that hour timed in eternity? We understand now why Jesus must "needs" pass through Samaria, and we realize that when God impresses us with a certain duty, we dare not evade it! Here is "the *must* of service." Peter must go to Cornelius, though, as a strict Jew, he had never entered a Gentile house. Philip must leave a great revival in Samaria and go to wait on a lonely road for the coming of a certain chariot. Paul must leave Ephesus on the left and Galatia on the right to make straight for

The "Must" of Service

Philippi. And every good man must allow his steps to be ordered by the Lord.

This woman evidently looked on religion as a matter of drawing up her supplies with difficulty from the pit of religious ordinances. Our Lord taught her that true religion was the upspringing of a perennial fountain. A careful reading of the text with the marginal references makes this distinction clear, and we also learn that we must not hide our secret sins when we are dealing with God. "Go, call thy husband and come hither!" This really meant that she must confess her sins and have them put away, before she could expect the uprushing of the fountain of life. Once in my experience the whole water supply of our college was cut off, because a frog, when a tadpole, had got caught in the joint between the house-pipe and the main, and, living on the water, had swollen into sufficient size to block all our supplies. Is not that a true parable? If anything questionable or wrong is being harboured in your heart, be rid of it, that again the fountain of life may begin to arise!

It is related of Grellet, the Quaker preacher, that he felt led to preach at a certain spot in a Canadian forest to the lumbermen, but on reaching the spot, he could discover no living person. However, he preached the sermon with the earnestness he would have expended on a crowd, and returned home, greatly wondering. Eight years afterwards, a man accosted him on London Bridge, saying that he had been looking out for him all that time to tell him that he had been foreman to the gang, that they had moved deeper into the forest, and he had returned to fetch some tools which had been left behind, and that, whilst looking for them, he had heard that sermon, which was the means of his conversion, and of all his fellows to whom he retailed it. Here was "the 'must' of service" and the result. God help us to be equally obedient to the heavenly vision! So shall "the 'must' of service" bring a Sychar to God!

The Eagerness of the Emancipated Soul

As we have seen, the woman left her waterpot! We can imagine the speed with which she went her way into the city with her new-found joy. She had been their sport, now she was their evangelist! The spring had overflowed within her heart and was demanding expression. She cherished no grudge against these men, some of whom may have helped to her downfall! Those who are one with Christ through the Spirit find themselves filled with a love that kindles a revival in other hearts as well as in their own. It was because of the love that glowed in this wondrously transformed soul that the Samaritans came to Christ, and invited Him to tarry with them. The love of God glowed in her heart, because she had put away her sin, and the spring of eternal love had begun to rise within.

In a large mining centre, during the Welsh Revival, the evening meeting was commencing in the crowded chapel an hour before the advertised time. Some were praying, some giving their experience, many were singing or reciting texts of Scripture. In the midst of the excitement, Evan Roberts entered, passed to his chair in the pulpit, and knelt for a time in silent prayer. His sensitive nature soon became aware that the meeting was stirred more by emotion than by the love and power of God. So he rose, silenced the hubbub, and for a whole half-hour made the great congregation remain hushed beneath the searching light of the Holy Spirit. At the end of that period, one of the best-known mineowners of the neighbourhood rose from his seat and extended his hand to another mineowner, and the two men, professing Christians, who had been at feud for years, were reconciled. Instantly, the entire atmosphere of the meeting was changed. The keynote was Calvary, and the power was that of Pentecost. Scores were born into the kingdom of God, and all were conscious of the overshadowing presence of the Saviour. Like one vast choir, the people sang a new song, and to those two men the blessed consciousness of God's love came at full tide. You must get right with God if you would have springing-water.

Open your nature to the Spirit of God! Let the spring rise, first in worship, and then in love, as with this woman. Love, which forgives and forgets, which harbours no self-will, cherishes no grudge, and meets the sharp edge of adverse criticism with gentle forbearance. Then mines of diamonds will open under your feet, and the river-sands will yield gold.

It was the habit of the late C. H. Spurgeon, when about to speak in a large auditorium, to detect "the chord of the place," because each place has its special note, and to speak in accord with this would enable him to speak without strain. Now, the one chord which is sounding through the universe is the love of God. It is the keynote to which every harp touched by angel-hands is attuned. Its notes waft down to earth, and are caught by blessed souls, who, like this woman, have been unlocked by Christ. Therefore, little children, let us love, for love is of God, and they who abide in love abide in God, for God is love!

Where cross the crowded ways of life,
   Where sound the cries of race and clan,
Above the noise of selfish strife,
   We hear Thy voice, O Son of Man.

In haunts of wretchedness and need,
   On shadowed threshold dark with fears,
From paths where hide the lures of greed,
   We catch the vision of Thy tears.

O Master, from the mountain-side,
   Make haste to heal these hearts of pain.
Among these restless throngs abide,
   Oh, tread the city's streets again;

Till sons of men shall learn Thy love,
   And follow where Thy feet have trod;
Till, glorious from Thy heaven above,
   Shall come the City of our God.

FRANK MASON NORTH

THE "MUST" OF SPIRITUAL WORSHIP
AND OF
THE HOLY SPIRIT

John iv. 24

A PERSON . John xvi. 8 and Acts xv. 28
ALWAYS IN THE WORLD . . Gen. i. 2
AGENTS IN
- Regeneration . . John iii. 6
- Inspiration . . 2 Pet. i. 21
- Revelation . John xvi. 13, 14

DISTINGUISH BETWEEN —

REGENERATION AND ANOINTING 1 John ii. 27
THE ANOINTING OF OUR LORD . John i. 32
                                       Luke iv. 18
HIS PROMISE AND FULFILMENT Acts i. 4–8
                                       Acts ii. 33
RECEPTION BY FAITH . . Gal. iii. 14
THE CONDITION OF HOLY LIVING Gal. v. 25

THE HOLY SPIRIT

"*Most gracious Saviour, who, in Thine Ascension, didst claim and receive the gift of Pentecost for each member of Thy redeemed Church, help me to reckon on Thee as the power and endorsement of my testimony for Thee! May I walk in the Spirit, pray in the Spirit, bear witness in the Spirit! Thus may I, and those to whom I minister, grow in grace, and in the knowledge and love of God!*"

V

THE "MUST" OF SPIRITUAL WORSHIP AND OF THE HOLY SPIRIT

"God is a Spirit: and they that worship Him must worship Him in spirit and in truth."—JOHN iv. 24

BECAUSE of its absolute importance, I repeat what we have already discussed. Whatever was stated in our first chapter is of critical importance to this present one. The soul, which is the centre of our personality, can operate in two worlds. From its level we can ascend into union with the Unseen and Eternal *through the spirit* or may descend into union with the earth *through the body*.

Let this be deeply pondered! It is the secret of all true thinking! The *soul* is you, or I, or any other. The reason, affections, emotions, judgment, gift, business-faculty, the love of the beautiful and true, have their home there. But the soul looks out on two spheres. To the *invisible* sphere it is related by the spirit, with its spiritual organs of touch, hearing, taste, and its quick scent in the fear of the Lord. In the *visible* sphere it is related to the body, with the corresponding physical organs of sight, touch, hearing, taste, and scent. We have the option of ascending by the upward staircase to fellowship with God, or descending by the downward staircase of the senses into materialism, self-indulgence, and hell. The ladder reaches to heaven, to which, as Jacob saw, angels ascend or descend, or the lure of savoury pottage attracts Esau to barter away his birthright.

According to the apostle's teaching in 1 Corinthians ii. 14, 15, there are multitudes who never rise above the natural or soulish level. Like the first Adam, after the fall, they are living souls, but they know nothing of "the last Adam, who is a life-giving Spirit." They bear the image of the earthly; and die without having been lifted, through the obedience of faith, into union with the heavenly Man, the Lord Jesus Christ. They are unlit candles. The inner chamber of their nature has never been illuminated by the Shechinah. The throne-room has never been occupied by the King. The windows that look out on the Delectable Mountains and the City of God have never been unshuttered.

But all this is altered when the soul turns to God in faith and obedience. *Then* we are born into a new world! *Then* we become aware of the Unseen and the Eternal, as we used to be of the passing shadows of time and sense. *Then* the spiritual senses, which we have enumerated above, become as quick to discern good and evil as our physical senses to distinguish light from dark and sweet from bitter. The Shechinah shines in the Most Holy Place! The King ascends the throne! Our real life is hidden with Christ in God; and through the open windows we look out on the things prepared for those who love God. By faith in Jesus, as we have already seen, we are born into the family of the first-born, whose names are written in heaven! Just as the human hand, when stretched out, has two sides, the one towards heaven, the other towards earth, so the act of entrance into this blessed life has two aspects. The angels describe it as being "born from above"; men call it "trusting Jesus." Two aspects of the same experience. If you are trusting Jesus, you are born from above. If you are born from above, you will be trusting Jesus (John i. 12, 13).

When the human spirit has been thus vitalized, the soul begins to worship God in spirit and in truth. This was the burden of our Lord's closing words with the woman at Sychar's well!

Do We Worship Enough?

Our Saviour tells us that the Father "seeketh" such to worship Him; and the grave question for us all is whether He ever bends over us, as we kneel, receiving as grateful incense the ascriptions of our worshipping love. He hears us voluble in petitions, which we may have uttered for years! He hears our intercessions for others, which are the expression of human affection! But does He often hear the outburst of worship and praise from hearts which have obeyed the Psalmist's injunction to join the universal chant arising from the unfallen universe? To this the Psalmist calls us, when he says, "O come, let us sing unto the Lord; let us make a joyful noise to the rock of our salvation. O come, let us worship and bow down; let us kneel before the Lord our Maker."

Let us kindle our hearts to praise by listening, as Isaiah did, to the chant of the seraphim—" Holy, holy, holy, is the Lord of hosts, the whole earth is full of His glory "; or by listening to the song of the Virgin-mother: " My soul doth magnify the Lord, and my spirit hath rejoiced in God my Saviour "; or by listening as John did to the out-circling song of heaven, beginning with the inner circle of the redeemed, and reaching out to every created thing, which is in the heaven, and on the earth, and on the sea: " Unto Him that sitteth on the throne, and unto the Lamb, be the blessing, and the honour, and the glory, and the dominion. And the four living creatures said Amen! and the elders fell down and worshipped."

In order to incite our sluggish souls to worship,

The " Must " of Spiritual Worship 67

we may recite aloud the Psalms, or the Te Deum, or any of the great hymns of the Church. But, best of all, it is for the soul to pour out its adoring gratitude and love in its own glad words. " We give Thee thanks for our creation, preservation, and for all the good things in our lives, but above all for the redemption of our world by our Lord Jesus Christ and for our own adoption into eternal union with Thyself."

In order to have spiritual worship and power, we need the presence and power of the Holy Spirit to quicken our spirit with His life-giving energy!

We need not take time to prove that the Holy Spirit is one with the Father and the Son in the Holy Trinity. His personality is proved by John xvi. 8, 13, and by Acts xv. 28. He has been in the world from the beginning (Gen. i. 2). Through His inspiration, the holy men of old were moved to write the Holy Scriptures (2 Pet. i. 21). It was beneath His mighty influence that the mountain-top saints and heroes of the past wrought and spake. They were elect souls, who dwelt apart, breathing the rare air of God's highlands. The full mystery of Pentecost was not unveiled to the majority of these men, though Joel foresaw the time when the Spirit would be poured out *upon all flesh*, when sons and daughters would prophesy, when old men would dream dreams, and young men would see visions, and when on servants and handmaids would be poured out the same Spirit. Then the valleys would be exalted! Then the gifts of an Elijah, a Jeremiah, a John the Baptist would be shared by an ever-increasing multitude of happy souls. That was the meaning of Pentecost. To us, also, it has been revealed that the Gentiles may be fellow-partakers in the joy, triumph, and power of the Spirit's fulness! As the glorious result of our Lord's Ascension, in our nature, to the right hand of God, the full power of the Holy Spirit is within the reach of the simplest, humblest souls, who are joined to Him by a living faith. The farewell discourses prove that it was His clear intention through His Ascension to claim for His whole Church—the mystical Body—the same anointing of the Spirit as He had Himself received at His baptism, when He said "the Spirit of the Lord is upon Me, and He hath anointed Me to preach." The oil that anointed the head of our Great High Priest was intended to fall on us also, who are but as the hem of His garment.

THE PATHWAY OF CHRIST'S ASCENSION

Linking together Luke xxiv. 50, 51'; Acts i. 9, 10; Ephesians i. 19–23; we gather that when the cloud hid our Lord from view, as the veil fell behind the high priest on the Day of Atonement, He was beset by the concentrated opposition of hosts of evil spirits, as though they resolved to bar His way. It was a vain attempt. His course was no more interrupted than the course of a sunbeam can be arrested by a flimsy veil of mist. He ascended on high, leading captivity captive. As in the triumphal progress of a Roman conqueror, his car was followed by a long train of subdued princes and warriors, whom he had defeated, and who would presently be put to death, so we may picture death, the grave, and principalities and powers of evil following in our Saviour's return to heaven. "Having put off from Himself the principalities and powers, He made a show of them openly, triumphing over them in His Cross" (Col. ii. 14, 15).

May we not here make use of the magnificent symbolism of the ancient psalm (Ps. lxviii. 17, 18), quoted by the apostle in Ephesians iv. 8? The chariots of God came forth to welcome the returning King "even thousands upon thousands"; and they turned to accompany His progress as He approached the celestial city. We hear the challenge of the foremost ranks, "Lift up your heads, O ye gates, and be ye lifted up, ye everlasting doors, and the King of Glory shall come in." To the inquiry "Who is the King of Glory?" the entire crowd of rejoicing angels and jubilant saints reply, "The Lord strong and mighty, the Lord mighty in battle!" Then the celestial doors slowly open to receive Him. He bears the semblance of our humanity! He is the man Christ Jesus! But on His vesture and on His thigh, He hath a name written, *King of Kings, and Lord of Lords.* Our Saviour promised "I will pray (or make request of) the Father, and He shall give you another Paraclete, that He may be with you for ever" . . . "even the Spirit of truth," . . . "which proceedeth from the Father." . . . "If I go, I will send Him unto you" (John xiv. 16, 17, xv. 26, xvi. 7). It is as if, on entering the presence-chamber, when the Father asked Him what reward He desired for His obedience to the death of the Cross, He replied, "Father, I ask nothing for Myself! But that Thou shouldest grant that by My divine human nature I should be the channel of communication to My Church, and through her, of that same Spirit, which Thou bestowedst on Me in My earthly ministry, that they all may be one, as We are!"

The Gift of the Ascended Lord

Peter tells us in his Pentecostal sermon that being by the right hand of God exalted, Christ received from the Father into His divine human nature that

The "Must" of Spiritual Worship 71

same fulness of the Holy Spirit, which He had shared from all eternity and now poured forth as His wonderful gift on His waiting Church. The apostle was so conscious of this—which probably the Master had promised and explained during the forty days—that he proceeded to announce that this gift was intended, not only for Jews, but also for Gentiles, even as many as the Lord should call to Himself (Acts ii. 39).

It pleased the Father that in Him, in His mediatorial and representative capacity, equally as in His deity, all the fulness of the Godhead should dwell. To each of us a share in that gift has been apportioned. The Father does not give by meter or measure (John iii. 34). Our cup was meant, not only to be filled, but to run over. Whether we have claimed it or not is another matter. Too many are content to claim their share in Calvary, but never go further to claim their portion in the gift of Pentecost. They are content with the brazen altar and the laver, but never enter the holy or the holiest place.

It is when we have claimed and received our share in the gift of Pentecost, that we can most readily realize the ideal of worship which our Saviour presented to this woman. It is only as we live in the Spirit and walk in the Spirit, that we are lifted into that consciousness of adoption, of those heavenly places, and of that power of service, which characterizes the sons and daughters, the witnesses and ministers of Christ's Holy Gospel!

There is a land, a happy land! Not "far, far away," as we were taught in our childish hymn; nor after death, but here and now! Bunyan called it "The Land of Beulah." There, God's glory ever shineth; the waters never become exhausted or stale; and the flowers bloom in a perpetual spring. They who dwell there need no candle, neither light of the sun, nor of the moon, for the Lord God is the everlasting light, and the days of mourning are ended. There, to us also, as we look North, South, East, and West, God says, "Arise, walk through the land in the length of it and in the breadth of it, for unto thee will I give it." There we meet the saints of every age! There God wipes all tears from all faces! There we have the foretaste of what is yet to be realized when the earth that is now, and the time-sphere, and the fading phantasms of the present, have passed away as a dream, and have given place to the new heavens and the new earth born out of the travail of the present! We shall have no reason to be disappointed, and God will not be ashamed, when we see that City which He has prepared, beyond the storm-clouds of the last black night of time! But of all this we get foregleams, as

The " Must " of Spiritual Worship

John in the isle of Patmos, when he was in the Spirit.

Can we be surprised that the woman forgot her waterpot, and ran at full speed to the city! When we have the Holy Spirit as a spring rising in our hearts, we no longer require our waterpots! No more the letting down of the pitcher, but the music of the spring arising from the depths of divine love! Yes! Paul! You were right when you said that eye hath not seen, nor ear heard, nor the heart of man conceived the things which God hath prepared for them that love Him, but He has revealed them unto us by His Spirit (1 Cor. ii. 9, 12, 14).

Two Closing Cautions

(a) We must carefully avoid making the Holy Spirit the figure-head in any movement, however sincere and well-intentioned its promoters may be. It is surely a profound mistake to make any special experience of the Spirit the objective or aim of a religious movement. In the present dispensation, the one aim of the Blessed Paraclete is to glorify our Saviour : and He must surely shrink from any attempt, however well intended, to divert one thought from Him, who must ever be the Alpha and the Omega of our faith.

(b) A recent movement has led to such excesses

that it is wisest to avoid it and similar movements, unless the promoters observe the following principles laid down in 1 Corinthians xiv. 27-29:

1. Those who profess to speak with tongues must, as their objective, seek only the glory of Jesus, the edification of the Church, and the convincing of unbelievers.

2. They must distinguish between physical contortions which may be matched by the Mohammedan dervishes—who run skewers from cheek to cheek and inflict horrible wounds—and the Spirit, which ever glorifies our Lord.

3. They must, before uttering their message, be sure that an interpreter is present.

4. They must control their own witness and keep silent if three others have spoken.

5. The women are not to speak in the meetings, but wait till they get home. "It is a shame for women to speak in the church."[1]

Whatever rends and divides the Church carries on its front the brand of Satan! Love must rule!

[1] But this does not prevent their speech in evangelistic gatherings.—F. B. M.

If we with earnest effort would succeed
To make our life one long, connected prayer,
As lives of some perhaps have been and are;
If never leaving Thee, we had no need
Our wandering spirits back again to lead
Into Thy Presence, but continued there,
Like angels standing on the lighted stair
Of the sapphire throne, this were to pray indeed
But if distractions manifold prevail,
And if in this we must confess we fail,
Grant us to keep at least a prompt desire,
Continual readiness for prayer and praise,
An altar heaped and waiting to take fire
With the least spark, and leap into a blaze.
ARCHBISHOP TRENCH

THE DAY OF PENTECOST

Acts ii. 1-47

THIS WAS THAT
THIS IS NOT THAT
THIS MIGHT BE THAT
THIS SHALL BE THAT
HOW THIS MAY BE THAT

THE DAY OF PENTECOST

"*Most gracious Lord! Thou wast anointed of the Holy Spirit for Thy glorious ministry; so deal with us, and with Thy whole Church, that we also may all receive the unction of the Holy One and be Thy witnesses!*"

VI

THE DAY OF PENTECOST

"*This is that.*"—ACTS ii. 16

WE need not stay to prove the personality of the Holy Spirit. If it were in question, a decisive answer would be afforded by the wording of the circular letter sent from the first Church Council to the daughter Churches, which were awaiting guidance. The epistle begins with the august and significant words, "It seemed good to the Holy Spirit and to us." The obvious interpretation of such an inscription is the equal personality of the Holy Spirit with that of the assembled leaders of the Church. He came to act as the executor of the Godhead, the conservator of the truth, the Lord and giver of life. The Day of Pentecost has been described as, in a sense, His birthday—*dies natalis*! His mission was to constitute the Church, as the Body of Christ, to rule and guide it, to add to it those that were being saved, and to reveal to them things which eye hath not seen, nor ear heard, nor the heart of man conceived, but which are made known to the Spirit-led.

I have sometimes wondered whether the good

Barnabas may not have crossed from his estate in the neighbouring isle of Cyprus, to spend a few days with his sister whose house had, not improbably, been the scene of the Last Supper, held in one of its upper rooms. His sister, Mary, at the dawn of the Day of Pentecost, would be early away from the home to the gathering of the disciples. Her brother and his nephew Mark might have been taking their early meal together, at which Rhoda was serving them, when suddenly a startling sound burst on their ears. Hastening from the house they ran out into the street, supposing that a terrific whirlwind had swept down upon the city. But to their surprise not a single leaf was quivering, not a tree was swaying. The sound had been that of a violent blast of wind; but clearly this was not the explanation. We may, therefore, imagine the two men joining with the crowds, as they streamed up the temple-steps under the impression that the mysterious sound was in some way associated with a divine epiphany. On reaching the temple court they found it crowded with a vast assemblage of at least three thousand people, Jews and proselytes, residents in Jerusalem, and visitors gathered from every quarter of the Empire. Here and there were little groups, each eagerly listening to a discourse in their own language, emanating from lips that seemed touched with a coal of fire! Finally,

The Day of Pentecost 79

however, these smaller circles became merged in one great audience, awaiting an authoritative explanation from the leader of the inner group, whose faces were illumined by a light that never shone on sea or shore.

May we not suppose that Barnabas would seek an explanation of this astonishing scene from a bystander, who might answer in some such words as these, " Clearly you are a stranger in the city, or you would not need to ask that question. This scene is closely related with the history of a wonderful movement, which for the last three years has engrossed the attention of the entire country. Of this movement one known as Jesus of Nazareth has been the central figure. The eminent purity of His character was combined with an extraordinary wealth of miraculous power, and He had become the idol of the people, especially in the northern districts of this country. Finally, He excited the jealousy of the priestly order, who, seven weeks ago, got the Roman authorities to crucify Him. But the extraordinary fact is that, to many of us, He has given certain evidence that He arose from His grave, and is still ministering to the needs of men. He promised that He would take steps to enable us to carry on the work which He commenced, but if you will listen to yonder speaker, you will learn all the facts at first-hand."

Here John Mark might break in and further explain to his uncle what he had heard from his mother of Peter's past history, and his close association with Jesus of Nazareth.

After dismissing the absurd charge of drunkenness, since the day was still young, the speaker commenced his main address by saying, "*This is that.*"

What was "This"?

For ten days the one hundred and twenty loyal souls had been awaiting the gift of spiritual power which their Lord had promised. Each day as it passed witnessed the same absorbed expectancy. "Not many days," the Lord had said, and therefore any day might be the one on which His gift might be poured forth. For the world's sake and for their own they had continued to claim the fulfilment of the promise and to rid themselves of every conceivable obstacle to its reception. It would appear that on this special day, when, in the temple, the priest presented the first loaves of the new harvest to the Almighty, they had risen from their knees, and were sitting in an expectant attitude. Then, suddenly, they saw tongue-like flames distributing themselves, one resting on the head of each, and they were all similarly anointed and filled with the Holy Spirit. The same experience befell

The Day of Pentecost

them as had befallen their Divine Leader when He was baptized. That had been His Pentecost, as this became their Baptism. Each looked at the rest, admiring their halos of fire, not daring to suppose that he or she was also similarly blessed From the beginning the Holy Spirit had brooded over the chaos of the elements and the ordering of human society; but, now, for the first time, as we have seen, He created the nucleus of the Body of Christ, and laid the foundations of the one holy mystical Church! This was according to Christ's word: "I will build My Church, and the gates of Hades shall not prevail against it."

"That"

"*That*," on the other hand, was the prediction of the Prophet Joel, who foretold that the hour would come when men-servants and maid-servants would break forth into prophecy; and that, amid the convulsions of nature and the fall of empires, vast numbers would call on the name of the Lord, and crowd through the gates of salvation. Peter in the scene before him perceived and declared the actual fulfilment of that ancient prophecy.

If Barnabas were there that day, he must have been deeply moved. The name, "Son of consolation," by which he was afterwards known, suggests his highly strung and tender nature; and he must have been very sensitive to the warm waters of love, which seemed to be let loose over that spellbound assembly. He had never experienced the like of it before. Here was that comfort in Christ, that fellowship of the Spirit, those tender mercies and compassions, of which he was so often to hear from the lips of his old comrade, Paul, in the university of Tarsus, as in after years they travelled together in the power of the same Spirit. His descent on the infant Church was being accomplished before his eyes.

Thus was fulfilled the Saviour's promise that they should receive power—the power of the Holy Spirit coming upon them.

" This " is not " That "

But we sorrowfully confess to-day that " *This* " *is not* " *That*." The professing Church, as we know it, is far removed from her Pentecostal prototype. " *That* " was united; " *This* " is divided into an infinite number of sects. " *That* " was full of triumphant joy; whilst " *This* " gets choirs and choristers to sing for her. " *That* " made little of material wealth; " *This* " pays court to it. " *That* " was characterized by simplicity of method, as each member said to neighbour and brother, " Know the

The Day of Pentecost

Lord "; whilst "*This*" substitutes paid agents to perform the work of evangelization and soul-winning. "*That*" was a commonwealth of mutual helpfulness; in "*This*," class distinctions are permitted and observed. No greater contrast between "*That*" and "*This*" could be adduced than between the brief sentences which describe the Church's infancy, when the Lord added to her *daily* those who were being saved, and the endeavour of modern Christian communities to attract audiences by an ornate ritual, or popular orations on the topics of the day, or adventitious attractions which savour of the dancing academy or the club. When at Colombo, I read an extract from a Buddhist paper in which a correspondent cited such things as "the ruses" adopted in a Christian country to induce people to attend church. There are vast numbers of significant exceptions, where buildings are crowded, and the Gospel is still proved to be the power of God to salvation; but, speaking generally, with the facts of Church decline before us, we are sorrowfully compelled to confess that "*This*" *is not* "*That*."

"This" might be "That"

The apostle did not say that Joel's prophecy was fulfilled. He clearly realized that the scene before him was only the first instalment towards its fulfilment. The gift of the Holy Spirit has never been withdrawn; and indeed miracles are happening to-day in the hearts of sinners, which are as wonderful as anything that has ever taken place in the history of the Church. The river of God flows on in its glorious fulness, though the professing Church has removed from its banks, and is creating a new settlement on the edge of a desert. How disastrous is this experiment! It is very bitter to state the matter thus; very bitter to draw a distinction between the professing Church and the hidden Church; very bitter to suggest that any amongst us are forsaking the fountain of living waters for cisterns that can hold none! Yet an instant alteration might be effected, if only the leaders of the Churches, both ministers and laymen, and indeed the membership as a whole, would turn once more to those stores of blessing which await us in "the residue of the Spirit"!

The following notable instances encourage the faith that God's arm is not shortened that He cannot save, nor His ear heavy that He cannot hear:

One Saturday afternoon, Christmas Evans, the famous Welsh preacher, was ascending Cader Idris on his way to a preaching engagement on the following day. He records that he was suddenly "convicted of a cold heart," and as the road was lonely he tethered his horse, went some distance apart, and cast himself before God in an agony of self-despair. He confessed his own sins, and those of the Churches under his care. The fountains of the deeps within were broken up. His tears came thick and fast, followed by a baptism of love and power, which affected the whole of his subsequent ministry, and led to a revival of religion throughout the principality.

The Rev. C. M. Birrell of Liverpool, who was a fellow-student with Murray McCheyne, the Bonars, and W. C. Burns, once told me of a conversation which, when a young man, had passed between himself and the mother of W. C. Burns, in which she gave him the key to the great revival, which touched the whole of Scotland. When she went to her son's room in the early morning to call him to his breakfast, she found him lying on the floor where he had been all night, detained by the Spirit of God, and oblivious to the flight of time. " Mother," he said, " God has given me Kilsyth to-day." Yes, and not only Kilsyth, with one hundred saved that afternoon, but Scotland and then Inland China, where he and Hudson Taylor wrought together.

Sitting with D. L. Moody, in the porch of his home in Northfield one Sunday morning, he gave me the following experience. Shortly after his conversion, he took the big Market Hall in Chicago

86 Five "Musts" of the Christian Life

and gathered a vast crowd of hearers for his Sunday evening service, but with comparatively small results. A group of Christian women used to occupy the front seats, and as he descended from the platform they would say something to this effect, " Very good, Mr. Moody, very good ; but there is something better, and we are praying for you." He often questioned what they referred to. Wasn't the hall crowded! Were there not signs of God's blessing in renovated lives ? But, one summer afternoon, as he was passing along Fifth Avenue, New York, he felt that he must get alone with God. Going to the house of a friend, he asked for the use of a room that he might be alone. He put aside the offers of hospitality and refreshment, and locked the door against interruption. In that sacred hour, he yielded his whole being afresh to Christ, and received the baptism of power. On the following Sunday evenings, the Spirit of God moved his audiences with such mighty power that the women who had prayed for him, with tears and smiles, said, " Ah, Mr. Moody, you have got it now ! " That was the beginning of a ministry in the power of the Holy Spirit, which was destined to affect the world.

But, perhaps, the outstanding incident of all is that recorded of John Wesley on his return from his residence in America, which had not been

The Day of Pentecost

marked by any outstanding features. He met Peter Böhler, a Moravian, at a religious gathering in Aldersgate Street, London, and afterwards accompanied him to Herrnhut, where, on the invitation of Count Zinzendorf, the consecrated and missionary-hearted Moravian Church had found its home. It was there that he entered on the experience of Pentecost, and, on his return to London, invited the Aldersgate group to meet him one afternoon at the Moravian Church in Fetter Lane. At that memorable meeting, in addition to himself, were his brother Charles, Whitfield, and others whose names were destined to shine as stars. After they had continued for two hours in fellowship and prayer, they became conscious of the mystic presence of the Holy Spirit, and fell on their faces in reverent worship, after which they arose and sang the Te Deum. On the next morning, Whitfield took the early coach to Bristol, and the great revival, the celestial fire of which saved Britain from the false fire of the French Revolution, broke out.

"This" shall be "That"

Why should not every minister and Christian worker who reads these lines arrange to spend one day at least alone with God in quiet self-examination? Are we experimentally possessed of the

Pentecostal enduement ? Are we willing to pay the price of it ? Are we willing, if needs be, to surrender reputation, position, and even the favour of our immediate clientele, in order that the channel-bed may be cleared for the river of God ? There is a sense in which we have to lay at the feet of our Lord " life's glory dead," before we claim " life that shall endless be." But, be it remembered, that whatever we surrender on the physical or natural —" the soulish-level "—will be given back with enhanced power and beauty on the spiritual. The man who fell down the well, and in falling caught the rope, held on to the end of it till his strength gave out, and then found that he had only six inches more to drop so as to reach the bottom unhurt. How often we dread letting go ! But it is only when we have let go that we find peace and power.

Let us then take the following steps suggested by the saintly Andrew Murray :

1. I believe that there is a Pentecostal blessing to be received—the anointing of the Holy Spirit, and the enduement with power.

2. I believe it is for me.

3. I have never received it ; or, if I received it once, I have lost it.

4. I long and desire to secure it at all cost ; and am prepared to surrender whatever hinders.

5. I do now humbly and thankfully open my

heart to receive all that I believe my Saviour is waiting to give ; and even if there be no resulting emotion, I will still believe that I have received according to Mark xi. 24.

If there is any difficulty in making a full surrender (see step 4 above), I suggest that if you are not willing to give up the key of some special door, which you have hitherto kept closed against Christ, that you should tell Him that you are willing to be made willing, and cast on Him the responsibility of dealing with that special difficulty. When dealing with your own case or the case of others, the one matter that claims imperative and primary consideration is the will. When *that* takes Christ's side, you may trust Him to deal with every hindrance or sin ; and He will.

As to steps, I trust that I may not be charged with egotism if I reprint part of a tract by Dr. Chapman : " Two or three years ago Mr. Moody invited me to breakfast at his home in Northfield. I got to the house before the breakfast hour, and met Dr. Meyer beneath a great tree in front of the house. I said to him, ' What is the matter with me ? So many times I seem half empty, and so many times utterly powerless ; what is the matter ? ' He put his hand on my shoulder, and said, ' Have you ever tried to breathe out three times without breathing in once ? ' I wondered if he was referring to some new breathing exercise, so I said, 'I do not think I have.' 'Well,' he said, 'try it.' So I breathed out once, and then I had to breathe in again. Then he said, 'You must always breathe in before you can breathe out, and your breathing out must always be in proportion to your breathing in.' Then he said, 'Good morning,' and I went on into Mr. Moody's house. But I had had my lesson, and know that I had been trying to breathe out more than I had breathed in."

There must be a constant inhalation of the Spirit of Pentecost!

       I have felt
A presence that disturbs me with the joy
Of elevated thoughts ; a sense sublime
Of something far more deeply interfused,
Whose dwelling is the light of setting suns,
And the round ocean and the living air,
And the blue sky, and in the mind of man :
A Motion and a Spirit that impels
All thinking things, all objects and all thought.
And rolls through all things.
         WILLIAM WORDSWORTH

RECKON ON GOD'S FAITHFULNESS

Mark xi. 22

SAMUEL'S MOTHER
THE NOBLEMAN'S SON
PAUL IN THE STORM
RUTH AND NAOMI (SIT STILL)
RECKON FOR FORGIVENESS
RECKON FOR ANSWERS TO PRAYER
RECKON ON GOD'S GUIDANCE

RECKON ON GOD'S FAITHFULNESS

" O Saviour ! Teach me to turn from my own fickle and changeful heart, and count more absolutely, and constantly, on God ! May I learn not only to pray to Him ! Teach me to reckon on His faithfulness ! "

VII

"RECKON ON GOD'S FAITHFULNESS"

"And Jesus answering saith unto them, Have faith in God. For verily I say unto you, That whosoever shall say unto this mountain, Be thou removed, and be thou cast into the sea; and shall not doubt in his heart, but shall believe that those things which he saith shall come to pass; he shall have whatsoever he saith. Therefore I say unto you, What things soever ye desire, when ye pray, believe that ye receive them, and ye shall have them."—MARK xi. 22–24.

YEARS ago, Hudson Taylor called my attention to these words of our Lord, and told me of the immense blessing they had been to him, in the early days of the China Inland Mission. He said that on his return from his first visit to China, he was deeply impressed with the need to plant missionaries in inland China. Up to that time, they were principally located on the coast.

It seemed as though the Saviour said to him, "Hudson Taylor, *I* am going to envangelize inland China; if you will walk with ME, I will do it through you." The challenge and promise were gladly accepted, and before that faithful servant of Christ passed home, one thousand missionaries had commenced the work of inland evangelization.

The secret which he had discerned in these verses

was to *reckon on God's faithfulness*, and to believe that what was true of Abraham would be equally true of himself. " He believed in the Lord and it was counted to him for righteousness."

In 1 Samuel i. 18, we read of Samuel's mother, that after she had poured out her soul to God, asking that a son might be given her, she went her way, and took her place at the sacrificial feast with a happy composure on her face. " The woman was no more sad." If we knew all, I expect that we should discover that she felt no need to repeat her prayer, so sure was she that it had been granted, and that a child would be given. *She reckoned on God's faithfulness!*

In John iv. 50, the nobleman, who came up from the bedside of his dying boy to seek the Saviour's help, was so satisfied that his request had been answered and his son was living, that he turned back home immediately on having received the Saviour's assurance, " Thy son liveth." " The man believed the word that Jesus spake to him, and went his way." He was so sure that his petition was granted that he actually—as "*yesterday*" suggests—slept on his way back to Capernaum, so confident was he that there was no further need of anxiety. He reckoned absolutely on the Lord's assurance and knew that what He said must be so. He was not, therefore, at all surprised to learn from his servants on the following morning that the lad was recovered. *He reckoned on the Lord's assurance, and was at peace!*

In Acts xxvii. 25 and 34, the apostle, resting on God's assurance that He had given him the lives of all his fellow-passengers, was able to inspire such confidence in his fellow-passengers that all of them took their last meal together before casting the cargo of grain into the sea, and this, even before the daylight revealed the creek into which they could run the vessel. When once God had given him the sure word of promise, he felt that there was nothing more to do or fear. In other words, he *reckoned on God's faithfulness!*

In the beautiful story of Ruth, we have an illustration in human life of similar reckoning on the assurance of a trusted man! Late one afternoon, Naomi and Ruth, after a toilsome journey, reached Bethlehem. Probably the old home, vacated ten years before, had remained untenanted, and there they sheltered, depending for their food on Ruth's gleaning in the neighbouring fields. She met with good success, but the permanent improvement of their position could only come through some arrangement for her future. According to Hebrew precedent, she had a claim on a leading citizen, a near kinsman, who was universally respected, and whose presence in the village council was the guarantee of order and righteousness. Naomi's thought was constantly turning towards him, and she was rejoiced to learn that he was prepared to do all in his power to help them. The only difficulty lay in the attitude of a yet closer kinsman, who might assert his prior claim.

The solution of the matter had to be decided by the village council. Hour after hour passed in their leisurely formalities. In the meanwhile the two women awaited the verdict. The elder woman had faith in the care of God's providence and felt sure that all would be well. Ruth, who was sitting with her in their cottage, found it hard to be patient. She kept rising to her feet, going to the door, looking up and down the street, feverish with excitement and unable to contain herself amid the lights and shadows that chased each other across her heart. Finally Naomi could bear it no longer, and said, " Sit still, my daughter, sit still! We have put the matter into our kinsman's hands. We can certainly trust him. The man will not be in rest till he has finished the matter to-day. Sit still! Sit still! " So it befell! Presently there was a step along the street, and Boaz entered to say that all was settled. The next kinsman had withdrawn his claims, and the way was clear for him to adjust the property and the field, and to take Ruth in marriage. After the night of weeping came the morning of joy;

and Ruth understood what her future husband had meant when he spoke of her resting beneath the wings of the Shechinah. So these two women were able to sit quietly waiting, because they trusted on the faithfulness of man. When we have placed our cause and need in the hands of Christ, let us sit still, assured that He will not forsake nor fail! Sit still, my soul! Sit still! Rest in the Lord and wait patiently for Him!

These three illustrations of the rest and peace which enter the heart that has learned to trust divine or human faithfulness, if carefully pondered, will point the way that we must tread, when we are troubled as to the issues and results of our prayers. Hand your burdens over to God by an act of child-like faith. Then trust in Him, and dare to believe that He has assumed entire responsibility. Make known your requests! Leave them with God! Trust His faithful care, do all that needs to be done! Go your way in peace!

Reckon on God for forgiveness! Years ago, I met an aged man who said that each night, before he went to sleep, he confessed all the sins he could remember, in order, that if he should die in his sleep, he would be sure of going to God. "But," I said, "is that not a terrible slur on God's faithfulness?" Did He not say, "I will remember their sins no more." Surely on our confession of sins,

98 Five "Musts" of the Christian Life

He blots them out for ever! If we confess our sins, He is faithful and just to forgive them, and to cleanse them away for ever! If we continue pleading for forgiveness of the same sins, day after day, year after year, are we not imputing infidelity to our Heavenly Father? When God once forgives, He forgets! He casts all our sins into the depths of the sea. They will never be cast up upon the beach.

If my grandchildren break a valuable vase, during their holiday visit to my home, and come at once to confess their sorrow, I will, of course, gladly forgive, and treat them as though the accident had never taken place. But if, day after day, they come to confess the same accident and ask for forgiveness, would it not cut me to the quick? Should I not feel that they mistrusted my attitude and my word? And how deeply must it grieve God, our Heavenly Father, if, after all His assurances, we still ask Him to forgive the same sins! We may be sorry that we ever transgressed. Such contrition is perfectly consistent with the consciousness of forgiveness. Obviously, we must constantly examine ourselves when we come to prayer, as to the manner in which we have been thinking, speaking, and acting in the interval, in case there is need for confession of some recent sin. We are constantly needing to have our feet washed, *i.e.* recent contact with men and things; but, as our Lord said, "He that has once been washed, needs only to wash his feet, but is clean every whit." This, then, is our first lesson! Reckon on God's absolute forgiveness of confessed sin! And, at the same time, be equally careful to forgive others who may have sinned against you. Remember, also, the following verses—Mark xi. 25, 26.

Reckon on God for answers to prayer. When, once, thoughtfully, deliberately, and believingly, you have handed the matter over to God, you must dare to believe that He has taken it in hand, and that, though He may keep you waiting, He will not be at rest until He has finished it. "The Lord will perfect that which concerneth me: His mercy endureth for ever: He will not forsake the work of His own hands."

Prayer is the co-operation of the human spirit with the divine. As a slight noise will sometimes dislodge an avalanche, so the prayer of faith sets in motion the power of the ascended Christ. Believing prayer supplies the fulcrum on which God rests the lever of His omnipotence. In prayer there is union between the divine and the human, so that, as the human body of our Lord provided the channels along which the divine life-power was able to reach us, so the prayer of faith opens a wide channel by which God's grace and providence may come to man.

True prayer has two characteristics. *First*: we must allow the Holy Spirit to winnow away what is inconsistent with God's will to grant. We cannot impose our will on God, but must wait for the solution of our life problems, which He will most certainly grant, sometimes by a flash, at other times by the slow unfolding of His will. When we cannot solve our problem in our own way, we must trust Him to deal with it in a better way ; and He cannot fail. *Second*: we must cease to worry. However long the interval, however strong the combination of adverse circumstances, we may still our hearts, in the patience of unwavering faith, sure that our Lord will not rest until He has finished the matter in hand, which we have entrusted to Him. Never forget to reckon on God's faithfulness ! That anchorage will never fail to hold !

Reckon on God's guidance. There is an immense realm within us known as the subconscious self. It has been suggested that much of this is concealed from our own knowledge, as seven-eighths of an iceberg are concealed beneath the surface of the ocean. By our surrender to Christ, we give to Him the right of access to these hidden depths ; and we become presently aware that such and such a course is the direction which we are to take. Our action in this respect will be presently corroborated by circumstances and by the gift of needed faculty.

Let us recapitulate the instances we have already quoted! Paul, kneeling in the Temple, becomes aware that his life-work henceforth must lie among the Gentiles. Philip discovers that he must leave the revival, which has just broken out in Samaria, and wait on a wilderness track for a certain purpose to be hereafter disclosed. Paul arrives in Ephesus just after Apollos has left it. Catherine of Siena writes: " Henceforth, my daughter, do courageously and without hesitation those things, which, by the ordering of Providence, are put into thy hands; for, being armed by faith, thou wilt happily overcome all thine adversaries." Mary Fisher traverses land and sea to give her message to the Sultan, which he receives with much attention and gravity. Stephen Grellet preaches a sermon, in the heart of the forest apparently to nobody, which leads to hundreds being brought to the Saviour. Carey is impressed to go to India, Judson to Burma, John Williams to Erromanga, Mary Slessor to Western Africa.

Tens of thousands, whose biographies have never been committed to the public press, have felt and obeyed the urge of the Spirit, to their everlasting joy.

Our one act must be to wait on God further for guidance. We must keep our souls before Him, as a still lake. We must cast on Him the responsibility of opening the way, providing the funds, and inclining our friends to acquiesce. The route, the companionships, the minding of things we are called to leave, the preparation for those that lie before, must be absolutely committed to His loving care and guidance. Everything will then be deftly and abundantly arranged. " Roll thy way upon the Lord ; trust also in Him, and He shall bring it to pass " (Ps. xxxvii. 5).

From the experience of a long life, I urge that the best confidant and adviser is Christ Himself ! The wisest course is to place the whole case in His hands, asking Him to advise and control. He is " the Wonderful Counsellor," says the prophet. " Trust in the Lord with all thine heart, and lean not to thine own understanding," says the Book of the Wise. " In all thy ways acknowledge Him, and He shall direct thy paths." He may suddenly put in your way a sagacious and experienced friend ! You may overhear a conversation, or come on a paragraph in the newspaper, containing the very information required. The extraordinary series of events, which Samuel predicted as waymarks to Saul, will have their counterpart in your experience (1 Sam. x.). " Lo, all these things doth God work twice, yea thrice, with a man, to bring back his soul from the pit, and that he may be enlightened with the light of life." Outward incidents combine with the inner life, as the lighthouse gleams with the readings of the chart in the captain's room !

Don't worry ! Don't anticipate ! Don't fear ! Don't, like Saul, offer the sacrifice precipitately before Samuel arrives ! Sit still, my soul, sit still ! Jesus, whom thou hast trusted, will not fail thee ! He will not rest nor fail till He has finished that which thou hast committed to His care ! Reckon on the faithfulness of thy faithful Creator and Saviour ! He cannot fail thee !

" The soul that to Jesus has fled for repose,
 He will not, He will not, desert to its foes ;
 That soul, though all hell should endeavour to shake,
 He'll never, no never, no never forsake."

FELLOWSHIP WITH CHRIST IN SERVICE

"Lord Jesus, Thou hast said, 'Take my yoke.' I believe that Thou art willing to tread, beside me, the hard soil of this earth! May I share Thy ploughing and sowing here, that I may participate, hereafter, in Thy golden harvest."

VIII

FELLOWSHIP WITH CHRIST IN SERVICE

"The servants that drew the water knew."—JOHN ii. 9

THIS miracle preceded "the Five Musts" in order of time; but the lesson it teaches is perennially true; and those who have passed into the realm of the Spirit will find inspiration as they consider this first miracle.

Cana was a little village, inhabited for the most part by vine-dressers, who tended the vineyards on the hills that descended to the great plain of Esdraelon. We can almost see the little white homes, embowered in a wealth of luxuriant foliage, looking down on that famous battleground. Thither our Lord came, fresh from the scenes of John's baptism, together with the five disciples, who had been introduced to Him through His contact with John the Baptist. These may have been rather startled when they found themselves transplanted from the austerity of the Baptist, with his locusts and wild honey, into the scene of marriage festivities, which, according to Jewish custom, would extend over the afternoons and evenings of a whole week, the guests going to their homes and avocations during the day, and afterwards resuming their marriage festivities.

In all probability the family by whom the feast was provided was related to the Saviour's home and family at Nazareth. This would account for Mary's responsibility in the matter of provision. In any case, our Lord would receive a hearty welcome ; and, though the apostles may have been startled by the contrast between the innocent merrymaking and the simplicity and gravity of the Baptist, they must have been convinced that the simple naturalness of the wedding was quite consistent with the high ideals for which Jesus stood.

In Christian service certain great principles should be observed. We may find them all in this suggestive story.

(a) *Be careful to watch for the appointed hour!* " Mine hour is not yet come." Mary was probably about fifty years of age, and her head was becoming streaked with grey hairs. But probably there was a new light in her eyes and a fresh spring in her step. The tidings which had reached her from the Jordan valley had probably altered the whole outlook of her life. She had been told by some, of the celestial light that had gathered about the dear figure of Jesus as He had emerged from the river

Fellowship with Christ in Service 107

in which the Baptist had baptized Him. Others had heard rumours of a voice.

For thirty years she had been waiting for something to happen which would vindicate her honour and reward her husband for his noble action in screening her. Nothing of the kind had, however, happened, and Joseph had died. Now, at last, it seemed as though she was likely to witness great unfoldings, and when the servants — probably friends and companions of the bridegroom—told her that, in consequence of the group of men whom Jesus had brought, the wine was nearly exhausted, a new hope sprang up in her breast, and the conviction of miraculous intervention on the part of Jesus seems to have broken upon her heart. So she whispered to Him across the table that the wine was running short.

He was already aware of it, and addressing her by the same noble title that emperors would address to their queens, the Lord replied that He was carefully watching the dial, and waiting for the exact moment to present itself for His interposition. "Woman! Mine hour is not yet come!" Herein is a deep lesson for us all. We, apt to be too hasty and precipitate in our actions, need this reminder! We must watch as well as pray! Our eyes must be fixed on the hands of our Saviour, like those on the swift movement of the hands of master or mistress in the old Hebrew households. In the case of Lazarus, the Master remained two days longer in the place where He was. Let us never forget that to everything " there is a season and a time for every purpose under heaven." " It is good that a man should hope and quietly wait for the salvation of the Lord."

(b) *Be careful to do exactly as you are bidden!* Presently the Lord turned to the leader of the little group of volunteers who were waiting on the guests, and asked him to have the waterjars filled which stood near the entrance door of the home. This request was a severe test to their obedient faith. Each of those great waterpots would hold some twenty gallons, and they had already fulfilled their purpose, for, as we are expressly told, they were used for the Jewish rites of purification. As the guests entered, water drawn from them had been poured over their hands and feet, according to Eastern custom. The sand and heat and perspiration of the lands that lie beneath the fervid heat of the sun demand the frequent application of refreshing ablution. As probably by this time they were empty, it would involve no small amount of labour and time to draw sufficient water from some neighbouring well or spring. These men were also needed to attend on the guests. Surely the morrow would be time enough to fill those capacious jars,

Fellowship with Christ in Service 109

in anticipation of a fresh relay of guests. But notwithstanding all this, there was no hesitation, and since Mary had bidden them act on the Lord's command the servants instantly obeyed. Nor did they give half-hearted response, for we are told that they filled them up *to the brim*. So full were they that if a chance leaf, borne on the breeze, had alighted on the brimming contents of one of those great jars, it would have overflowed, and some drops would have spilled on the floor.

If you would serve Christ you must not only wait until He issues His biddings, *but you must obey exactly and immediately* the commands of the inner still small voice. It can be recognized, amid all the babel of other voices, by the fact that it never alters, never asks questions, but is always direct and explicit. Often it asks for an obedience which is against, or above, what we might naturally feel disposed to give. Listen to that still small voice—the voice of the Spirit of God, and, *whatsoever He saith unto you, do it*! Not yours to question why! Not yours to make reply!

They who respond with prompt obedience, and allow Christ to become their absolute master and director, become transformed into His likeness. Like the angels, they do His commandments, hearkening to the voice of His word. Stephen Grellet, we repeat, will preach a sermon in a forest, apparently to no audience; and find, eight years afterwards, that a man, hiding in the undergrowth, was converted by his discourse, and finally became an evangelist, through whom large numbers were led to Christ. " The wind bloweth where it listeth, but thou canst not tell whence it cometh or whither it goeth; so is every one that is born of the Spirit." Always remember that the inner voice will be accompanied, sooner or later, by the corroboration of outward circumstances. Peter's vision on the housetop was corroborated by the call from the street below!

(c) *Be careful, in the service of Christ, always to give brimful measure.* It may be a very small thing! To take a class of poor children; to pay a visit to a dying man or woman; to write a letter; to give a tract or a pocket Testament. To fill a jar of opportunity may be a very simple, common act; but it is more than likely, that, if done at the command of Jesus and in His fellowship, it may lead to a marvellous unfolding of God's purposes. Only do your bit with all your soul, and mind, and strength! Let there be no lacking on your side! It is amazing that the Lord should ask our help and honour us as His fellow-workers; let us prove ourselves worthy of His confidence!

Those jars were not filled apart from strenuous labour on the part of the servants. It was not a

Fellowship with Christ in Service

light matter for them to draw water from a neighbouring well, and fill those big vessels. But they were proud to co-operate with One whose name and fame were beginning to be recognized. So, also, the measure of our sacrifice will always be the measure of our success. Is not this the lesson which our Lord intended to teach? This shall occupy our thought more at length; but, in the meantime, let us see to it that we do our best in all service that we render. Never give a message without previous thought and prayer! Never take a class or engage in service to the school, the church, or the community, without putting your best into it! Never be content, like Gehazi, to place the prophet's staff on the face of death; but, like Elisha, lay yourself on the child, your mouth on the cold mouth, your hands on the child's hands—till the flesh of the child waxes warm. Give your best, your finest, your most loving, your brimming answer to any appeal made to you in the name of Jesus!

Then a wonderful thing will happen. It has happened in the experience of many of us! We may have spent a week in thinking out and preparing our address. We have filled the waterpot to the brim, but as the time approaches for its delivery we are compelled to feel that it is a very poor attempt, comparable only to water. But as we begin to speak, and see faces suffused with tears or eyes filled with new hope, we realize that the Master has been collaborating with us, and has turned the water into wine. "The servants that drew the water knew!" Only the Master and they were in the secret! But how beautiful it is, when there is a secret understanding between Jesus and the servant, who is endeavouring to serve Him. Our fellowship (or partnership) is with Christ. When we go fishing with Him, He shows us when and where we are to let down the net. Sometimes He seems to alter the net from one kind to another. Let it be our aim to enter more deeply into this holy compact! We will mend the net, cleanse it of weed, and let it down into the deep on the right side of the ship. We will fill the jars to the brim. Then let us reckon on Him to do His share. Let people forget the servant (and put him in a bracket) whilst all glory is given to Jesus.

We must admit, to our shame, that we sometimes suppose that we can give wine, as the result of our own effort. But as we pour it out we find it water, and the people go away uncomforted, uninspired, and unhelped. We all know the immense difference, when a sermon is filled with the unction and power of the Holy Spirit. The preacher is well-nigh forgotten in the transcendent results!

(d) *Be careful to remember at how great a cost the Saviour purchased the salvation you proclaim!* We

Fellowship with Christ in Service 113

cannot turn from this suggestive first miracle without recalling the words of 1 John v. 6: "This is He who came by water and blood; not by water only, but by water and blood." That verse is generally quoted as referring to a remarkable fact, which is recorded by the apostle:

"Howbeit one of the soldiers with a spear pierced His side, and straightway there came out blood and water. And he that hath seen (*i.e.* John, the narrator) hath borne witness, and his witness is true; and he knoweth that he saith true, that ye may believe."

The soldiers were surprised to find Him dead. It was unnatural that one in the prime of life should succumb so soon. They could not account for it, but, to prevent any mistake, with a spear, pierced His side. Why does the Evangelist stress the fact that there issued forth, following the withdrawal of the spear-head, the clot and serum which filled the cavity of the heart? This proved that our Lord had not died as the result of His crucifixion, but that His heart had been broken previously. Christian medical science informs us that that heart-break took place, almost certainly in Gethsemane, when the sweat of blood appeared on Christ's forehead, and bedewed the grass on which He lay. So terrific was the conflict between Him and the prince of this world, who wished to stop Jesus from dying, that the Saviour feared that He would die before He reached Calvary. Therefore we have it in Hebrews v. 7: "Having offered up prayers and supplication with strong cryings and tears unto Him that was able to save Him from death, was heard for His godly fear." In other words, He was saved from dying then and there, and an angel strengthened Him to go through those last agonizing scenes in which He achieved the salvation of us all!

Shall we not say with the great Christian hymn:

> "Let the water and the blood,
> From Thy riven side that flowed,
> Be of sin the double cure:
> Save me from its guilt and power!"

It is a beautiful privilege to work along with Christ, but we shall not serve in that blessed apprenticeship long, without learning this lesson, that He has no pleasure in service rendered to Himself or others, that does not cost us blood! This is characteristic of His own service to the world, and you will find that He will soon drop you out unless you are prepared, in your measure, to surrender yourself to the blood-letting, which alone counts in the service of humanity. As we look out on society to-day we can understand why so many lives are unhappy. They have never learned that the one secret of happiness is to give to the point of self-denial and self-sacrifice. As Phillips Brooks has

Fellowship with Christ in Service

put it: "They need something to happen which shall force them out on the open ocean of complete self-sacrifice. If only a slow quiet tide or a furious storm would come and break every rope that binds them to the wooden wharves of their own interests, and carry them clear out to sea! The soul that trifles and toys with self-sacrifice can achieve neither its true joy nor power. Only the soul that gives itself up for ever to the life of others can know the delight and peace which surrender gives."

This trace of blood in our actions is a matter that we can never talk about. When it is being shed, we must anoint our head and wash our face, that men may have no inkling of what is happening. Neither the right hand nor the left hand must know, or divulge the secret. It should be remembered, also, that we have no right to deprive wife or child of whatever is necessary. It must be a personal act, reacting on no one but yourself. *You* must be the one who gives the blood, not they! Keep happy and smiling! When Jesus was performing this miracle, there was no strain or effort, no wrinkle on His forehead, no cloud upon His smile! He drew no attention to Himself; needed no thanks, and stole away unrecognized, at least for the moment, as the giver. Of course there is no merit in such actions. The blood we shed cannot atone, cannot save, cannot cleanse! Only His blood can do that! But, also, it is true that the great soul-winners of the world, have faced the blood of martyrdom, and counted not their lives dear unto themselves!

The best wine is kept till the last! Yes, that is the habit of our dear Lord. The world puts the best on the table, *first*; but its best is soon played out and exhausted. The sparkle is gone from the youth, and the colour from the maiden's cheek. "Vanity of vanities, all is vanity!" One by one, as the pampered children of this world come to the end of life, they have confessed that the wells of water they have drunk were brackish, and that their iridescent bubbles were only soap and water. "The world passeth away, and the lust thereof: but he that doeth the will of God abideth for ever."

Our Lord is ever giving more and more abundantly, more and more richly. In heaven, after we have been with Him for an age, He will still be leading us to know more and more of the things which God hath prepared for them that love Him. He bends over us now with some such words as these:

"Grow old along with me,
 The best is yet to be;
 The last of life, for which the first was made!"

My Redeemer and my Lord,
    I beseech Thee, I entreat Thee,
Guide me in each act and word,
    That hereafter I may meet Thee,
Watching, waiting, hoping, yearning,
With my lamp well trimmed and burning.

.   .   .   .

O my Saviour, I beseech Thee,
Even as Thou hast died for me,
More sincerely,
Let me follow where Thou leadest,
Let me bleeding as Thou bleedest,
Die, if dying I may give
Life to one who asks to live,
And more nearly,
Dying thus, resemble Thee!
           HENRY WADSWORTH LONGFELLOW.

OUR KNOWLEDGE OF OUR SAVIOUR

" Lead me in Thy truth and teach me! Help me not only to serve Thee, but to sit at Thy feet. May I follow on to know Thee! Teach me to share the fellowship of Thy Cross and Grave, that I may one day see Thee take to Thyself Thy great power, and reign. Thus, finally, God shall be all-in-all!"

IX

OUR KNOWLEDGE OF OUR SAVIOUR

"*I count all things to be loss for the excellency of the knowledge of Christ Jesus, my Saviour.*"—PHIL. iii. 8

IT is a searching question for us all to decide, whether we are making enough of our personal contact and friendship with the Lord Jesus. Undeniably it is now in a glass darkly, and very different from that face-to-face communion which will be possible, when earth's curtains are drawn back; but nevertheless there is, according to Paul, even in this life an excellency of knowledge, to obtain which he was prepared to forgo the loss of all things. It would be indeed a distressing comment on the misused opportunities of our lives, if at the end we should hear Him say, sadly, to us as to Philip: "Have I been so long time with you, and yet hast thou not known Me?" Paul, on the other hand, was prepared to count all things but loss, if only he might gain Christ.

I. *The incidents of life furnish most valuable opportunities of knowing our Lord.* Perhaps it has been specially ordered and contrived for that purpose. Probably the angels, with all their opportunities, can never have such a knowledge of the Son of God, as we who have summered and wintered with Him for the longer or shorter span of human existence. In a mountainous country we are glad to avail ourselves of the companionship of a friendly guide, who knows each step of the way which we must take. As mile succeeds to mile and we discover his practical acquaintance with every difficulty, his dexterity, and resource; we come to a knowledge of him and a faith in him, which perhaps the inmates of his household cannot possess. We know by experience how exact is his knowledge, how keen his eye, how steady his step! So with the Saviour. At the beginning of life, we trust Him, because of what others may tell us of Him; but, as the years pass, we can say as the Samaritans of old, "We have seen Him for ourselves, and know that this is indeed the Saviour of the world." May we not go further and confess that often our Father allows our need to reach a climax of difficulty which is absolutely insoluble by any wit or strength of our own: and then we suddenly awake, like Hagar, when God opened her eyes, and she saw the well of water that saved Ishmael's life (Gen. xxi. 14–21)!

It was when Sennacherib came against Jerusalem with the full equipment necessary to scale the walls, that Isaiah and Hezekiah discovered that Jehovah was prepared to be "a place of broad rivers and streams," which would effectually prevent them from reaching the outward defences of the city. There was no natural river—Jerusalem was built on the mountains—but the eternal God became all that a river would have been, intercepting the attack of the foe. They needed no intercepting river, since God Himself would intercept the attack by His own glorious intervention (Ps. xlvi. 4; Isa. xxxiii. 21, 22).

It was only when Ezra, on the return of the Jews to Palestine, halted at the Euphrates, that he awoke to the peril of crossing the wilderness, inhabited by robber tribes. But, in answer to his prayer, Jehovah supplied their lack of a band of soldiers and horsemen. The perils of that desert journey revealed a side of His character which otherwise had escaped their notice (Ezra viii. 22).

The sisters at Bethany would never have known our Saviour, as the Resurrection and the Life, had mortal sickness not desolated their home with their brother's death. So, in after years, they were thankful to have had that sorrow, which led to such a revelation. Paul would never have known what Jesus could be, unless he had suffered that thorn in the flesh. His sufferings provided a new angle of vision.

Do not dread the dealings of God's providence! He is leading you by a right way! There are texts in the Bible which you would never have understood, and there are *provisions or grace you would never have used, if your life had been otherwise than it is!*

II. *Loneliness is an opportunity for our Saviour to make Himself known.* It was when the beloved apostle was alone on the isle of Patmos that he was "in the Spirit," and the Spirit revealed the Lord. Thereupon a fellowship began which opened the way to an Apocalypse. The ancient mystics went to the deserts in order to enter on that intimacy. But this is not necessary. Get alone! Let the silt have time to drop to the bottom! Allow time for the glare of the world to die out from your eyes! Be still from the voices of flattery, of hatred, and of the passing hour! He that hath Christ's commandments and keepeth them, he it is that loveth Him and such will be loved by Him and by the Father, and they will come to him, and make their mansion with him, until one of the many mansions yonder shall be his home for ever. (The same word is used in John xiv. 2 and 23.) Thomas à Kempis says: "Shut thy door upon thee and call unto Jesus thy love. When Jesus is nigh all goodness is nigh; but when He is not nigh all things are hard. If Jesus speaks one word, there is great comfort. To be without Jesus is a grievous hell, and to be with Jesus is a sweet paradise. If Jesus be with thee, no enemy shall hurt thee. It is a great craft for a man to be conversant with Jesus ; and to know how to hold Jesus is a great prudence."

When, therefore, you are lonely ; when, like John, on the Lord's Day, you feel as though you were exiled from His house ; when the Ægean of separation intervenes between Patmos and Ephesus ; when the prayers and hymns of the sanctuary are lost in the intervening distance, remember that your loneliness constitutes a strong claim on your Saviour. He will not leave you orphaned and comfortless. He will come to you. Though you may be passing through a valley of shadow, and lover or friend appears to have forsaken, the Good Shepherd will go at your side, armed with a crook to extricate you from the pitfalls and a club to beat back your foes ! He is an unfailing Friend !

III. *Hours of suffering and pain yield conspicuous opportunities for a deeper knowledge of our Saviour.* It has been truly said : " There is none other way to life and inward peace but the way of the Cross." This was specially marked in Paul's experience. He was always bearing about in his body the dying of Jesus. Poverty, persecution, ill-health, the hatred of the Jewish party—such were the deep waters that threatened his life. But, in all, he was " more than conqueror," *i.e.* he carried off the spoils of war ! True, he suffered for Christ, but Christ *suffered* with him. The Master was ever by his side. Thus he tells us that they who receive the abundance of grace and of the gift of righteousness, shall reign in life through the one Man, even Jesus Christ. So he received and so he reigned (Rom. v. 15, 17).

Do not shrink back when Jesus leads you into a dark chamber, or brings you to an operating-table. One, of whom I have direct knowledge, was called to go through a severe surgical operation He was told that it might endanger his life ; and he resolved that therefore he would not employ an anæsthetic, rendering him unconscious, as he desired to enter eternity, as his Master did, with an unclouded brain. When laid upon the operating-table, he was just able to look over its edge on the ground, and he saw there *two pierced feet*. He recognized them to be his Lord's, and knew that Jesus was standing there. So absorbed was he with that vision, that he was absolutely unconscious of pain. In fact, he was quite surprised to hear that the operation was over. In a surprisingly brief period he recovered and was completely healed ! May we not believe that that same Presence is beside our beds of pain ! The martyrs would sometimes ask not to be taken off the rack of torture, because the vision of the Son of God, walking, as of old, in the burning furnace, was so real, so ecstatic, so oblivious of suffering.

The thousands of sick folk, who were brought

Our Knowledge of Our Saviour 125

from every part of Galilee, revealed qualities in Jesus which would have remained unknown, had they not thronged Him! The leper revealed His purity; the paralysed, His nervous energy; the dying, that He was the resurrection and the life. Each was a prism to break up the rays of colour hidden in His pure manhood. So each trial or sorrow, which we share with Him, reveals, not only to us, but to the principalities in the heavenlies, some new phase of that wonderful Being who is the complement of the broken circle of our lives (Eph. iii. 10). Let us dare to rejoice, when the Master entrusts us with a lifelong sorrow, and ever rejoice, because it constitutes a new claim upon His ever-present help. "Be thou faithful unto death, sentry, at thy post! The First and the Last is with thee. As He passed through death to glory, *so shalt thou.*"

IV. *Hours of thirst give opportunities for a more intimate knowledge of our Saviour.* Had that woman of Sychar not been compelled by thirst, she would not have visited the well on the noon of that memorable day! Were it not for the imperative demand and prompting of the soul-thirst, men like Augustine would never have said that they were dissatisfied until they rested in God. If we were perfectly supplied from ourselves, we should never discover the heights, and depths, and breadth, and length of the love of Christ. There are those amongst us who have immense capacity for human love, but have never been married, have never been loved supremely, nor have borne children of their own. They have thirsted, that they might learn, as so many have done, the personal love of Jesus!

Will not this constitute part of the blessedness of heaven! It is written: "The Lamb which is in the midst of the throne shall be their Shepherd, and shall guide them unto fountains of waters of life; and God shall wipe away every tear from their eyes" (Rev. vii. 17). Yes, even in that life, there will be need of supplies from outside of ourselves. We shall never become independent of our dear Lord! As we know, we shall follow on to know! Like Newton, we shall always feel that we are as children gathering stones on the shores of a boundless ocean! When we have explored one landscape of heaven, we shall be led to another, and yet another. We shall never be self-contained! Never able to dispense with Christ! Deep will always call to deep! Always satisfied up to our present need, but ever conscious of the awakening of new yearnings and hopes. Beloved, now are we the sons and daughters of the Almighty! We know not what we shall be, but we know that eye hath not seen, nor ear heard, nor the heart of man conceived, what God hath prepared for them that love Him!

V. *When we are most deeply convicted of the sin and failure of our best efforts, we shall appreciate, as never before, the purity and redeeming love of the Saviour.* We recall the final beatitude of the ascended Christ, as it is given in the Revised Version : " Blessed are they that wash their robes, that they may have right to come to the tree of life, and may enter in through the gates into the city " (Rev. xxii. 14). Alas ! that we need to wash them so often ! It must be a more terrible thing than we realize, to be a sinner. We fail to realize what His friendship costs, because this is a world of sinners, and we have never been in an untainted atmosphere, or mingled with an unfallen race. The child, born in a leper colony, cannot realize what the childhood of an untainted childhood is. We know enough to make us repent in dust and ashes, and cry, " Unclean," as Isaiah did when he beheld the worship of the seraphim and heard them inciting each other to loftier songs. "One cried to another ! " But we have never breathed untainted air, or mingled with an unfallen race !

But we know enough to make our Saviour absolutely necessary for peace, strength, and salvation. We can understand what Augustine meant when he cried, *" O beata culpa ! "* " O blessed fault ! " We dare not sin, that grace may abound, lest we open again the wounds of Calvary ; but in our hours of deepest contrition we have glimpses into the heart of Christ which unfallen beings cannot share!

After all, there is only one thing which really matters! It is "the excellency of the knowledge of Christ Jesus our Lord." The world is filled with discord and strife, with imitation and make-believes, with shams and counterfeits. In the shadows of the approaching night it is difficult to discriminate between friend and foe, as between the different shades of colour. But there is no mistake about Jesus Christ. Amid all the "isms" of the present time, see that you do not lose Him, who is "the Way, the Truth, and the Life." Possessing Him, you have the key to each of these!

That, then, is our last word! Whatever else has been set forth in these pages, of Calvary, the Ascension, and Pentecost—all must be subordinated to the one object of knowing, loving, obeying, and glorifying Christ.

"Yes, through life, death, through sorrow and through sinning,
 He shall suffice us, for He hath sufficed;
 Christ is the End, for Christ is the Beginning!
 Christ the Beginning, for the End is Christ!"

"I am Alpha and Omega, the First and the Last, the Beginning and the End!"